THIS BOOK

BELONGS TO:

- - - - - - - - - - - - - - - - - - - -

- - - - - - - - - - - - - - - - - - - -

- - - - - - - - - - - - - - - - - - - -

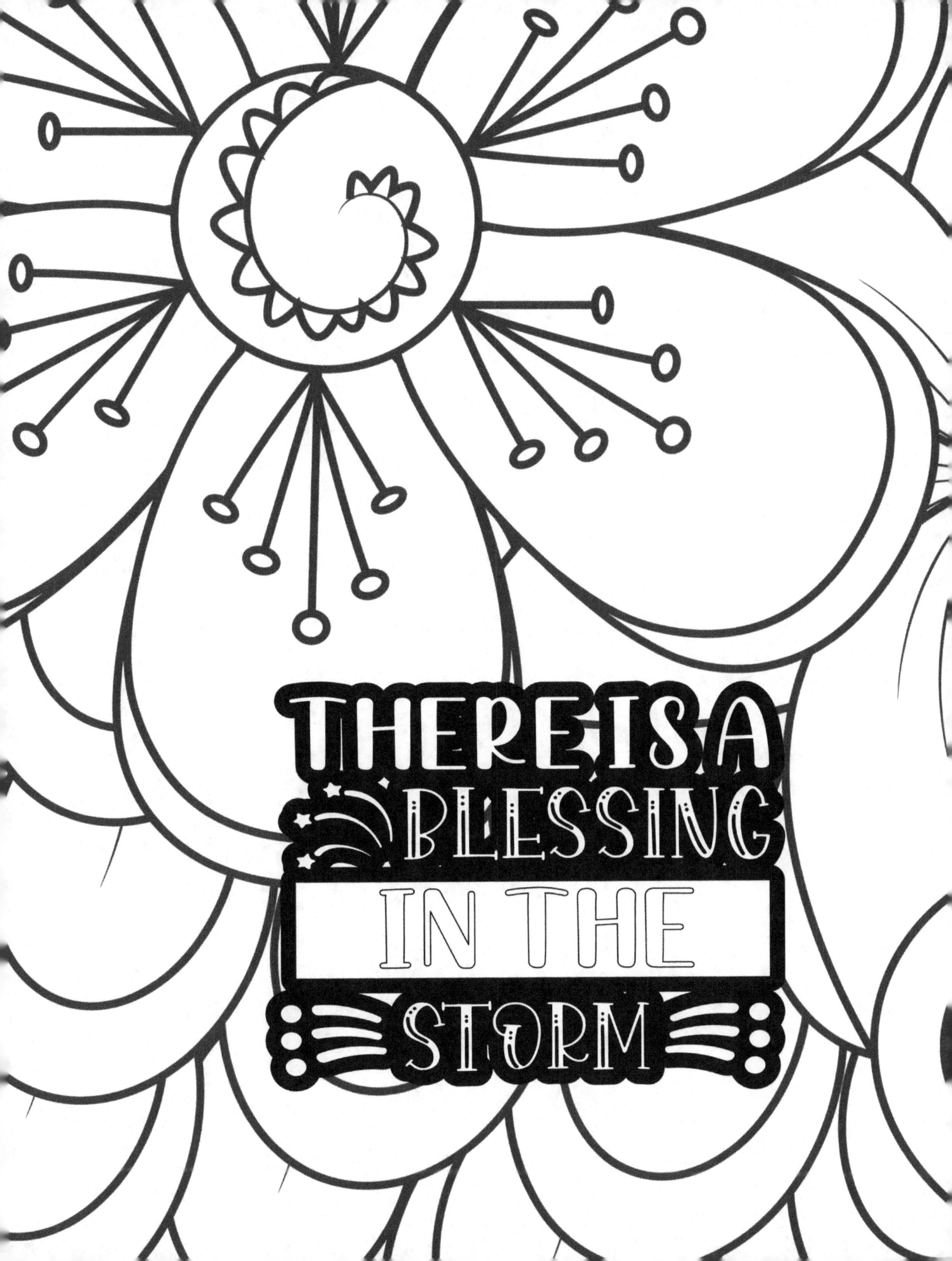
THERE IS A
BLESSING
IN THE
STORM

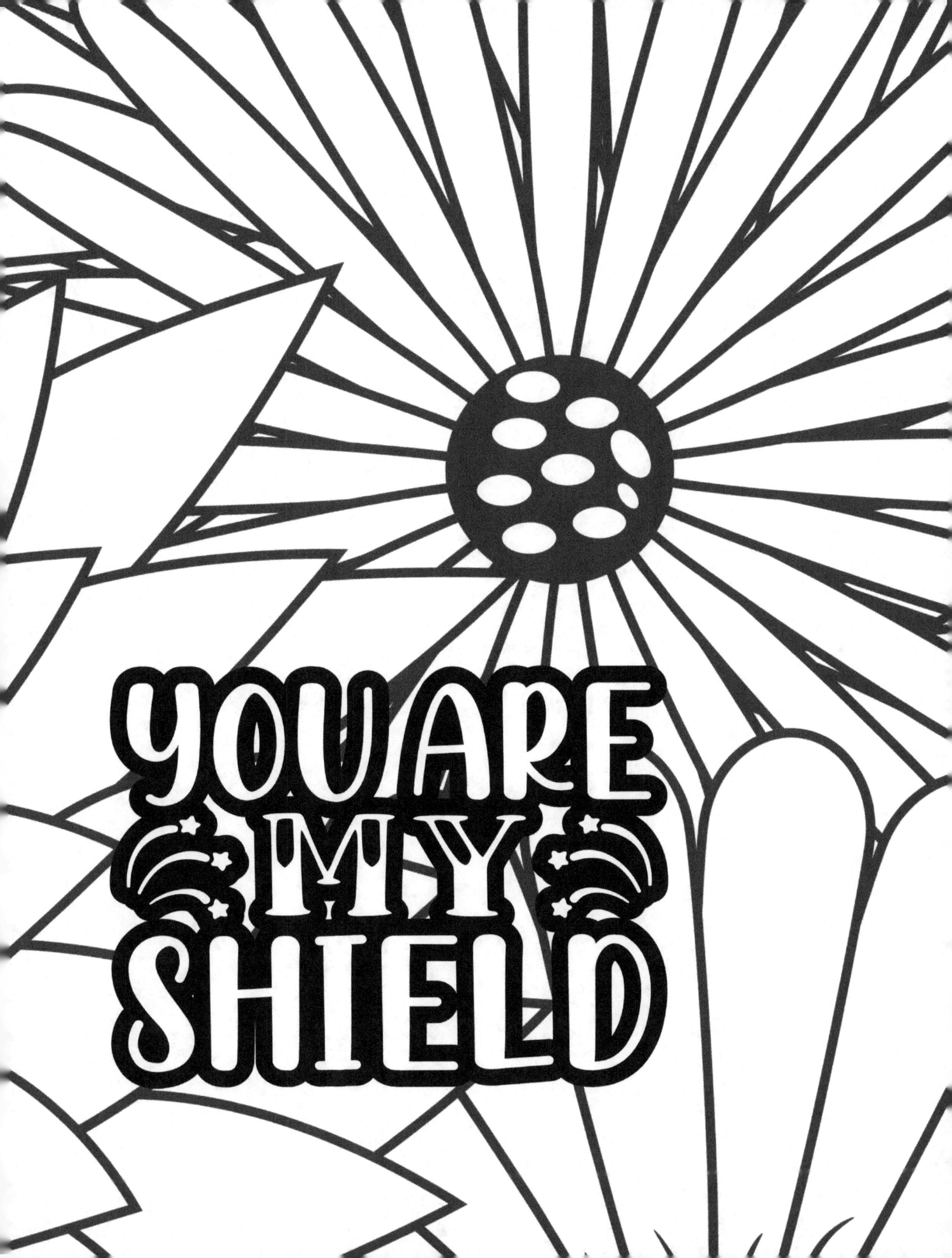
YOU ARE
MY
SHIELD

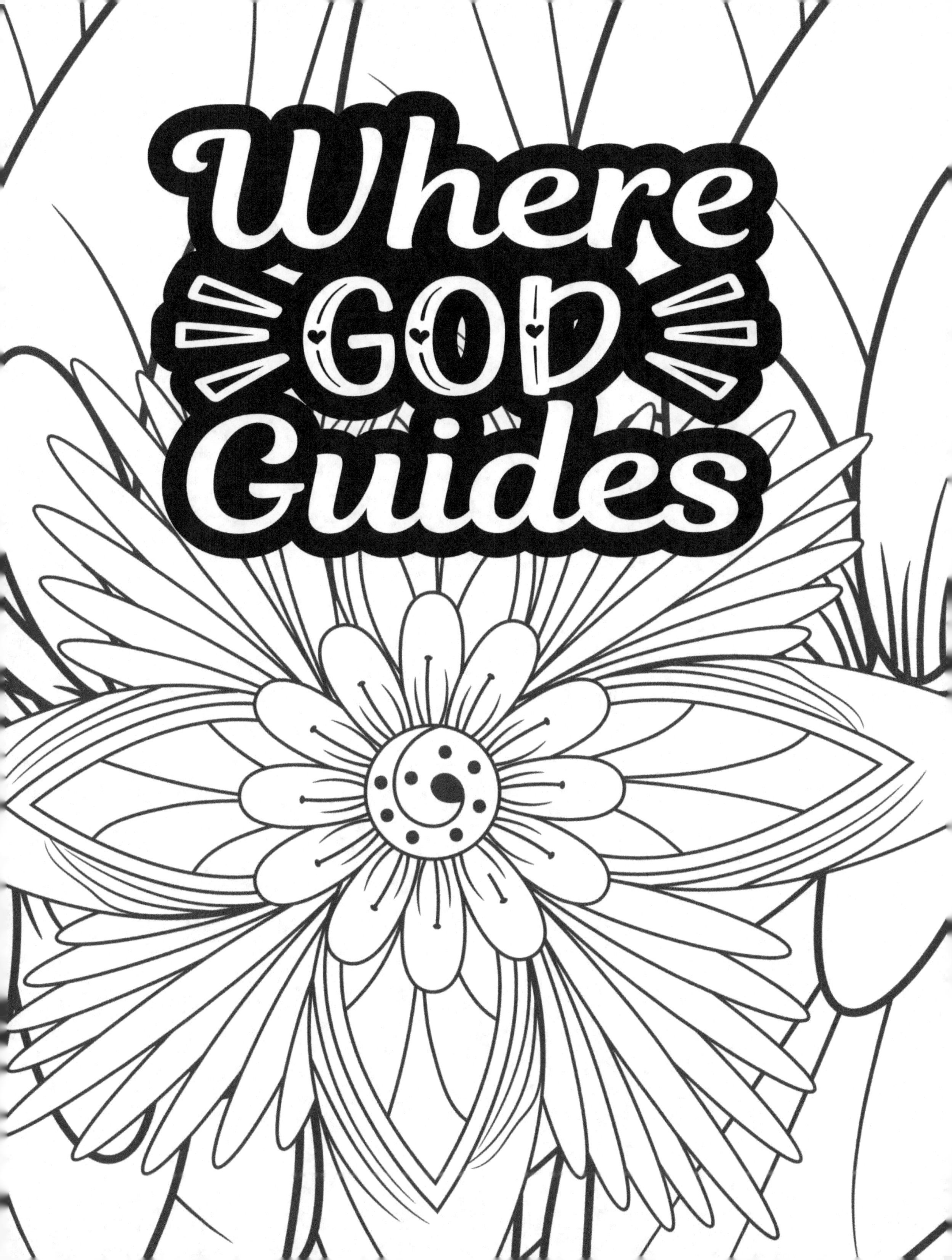
Where
GOD
Guides

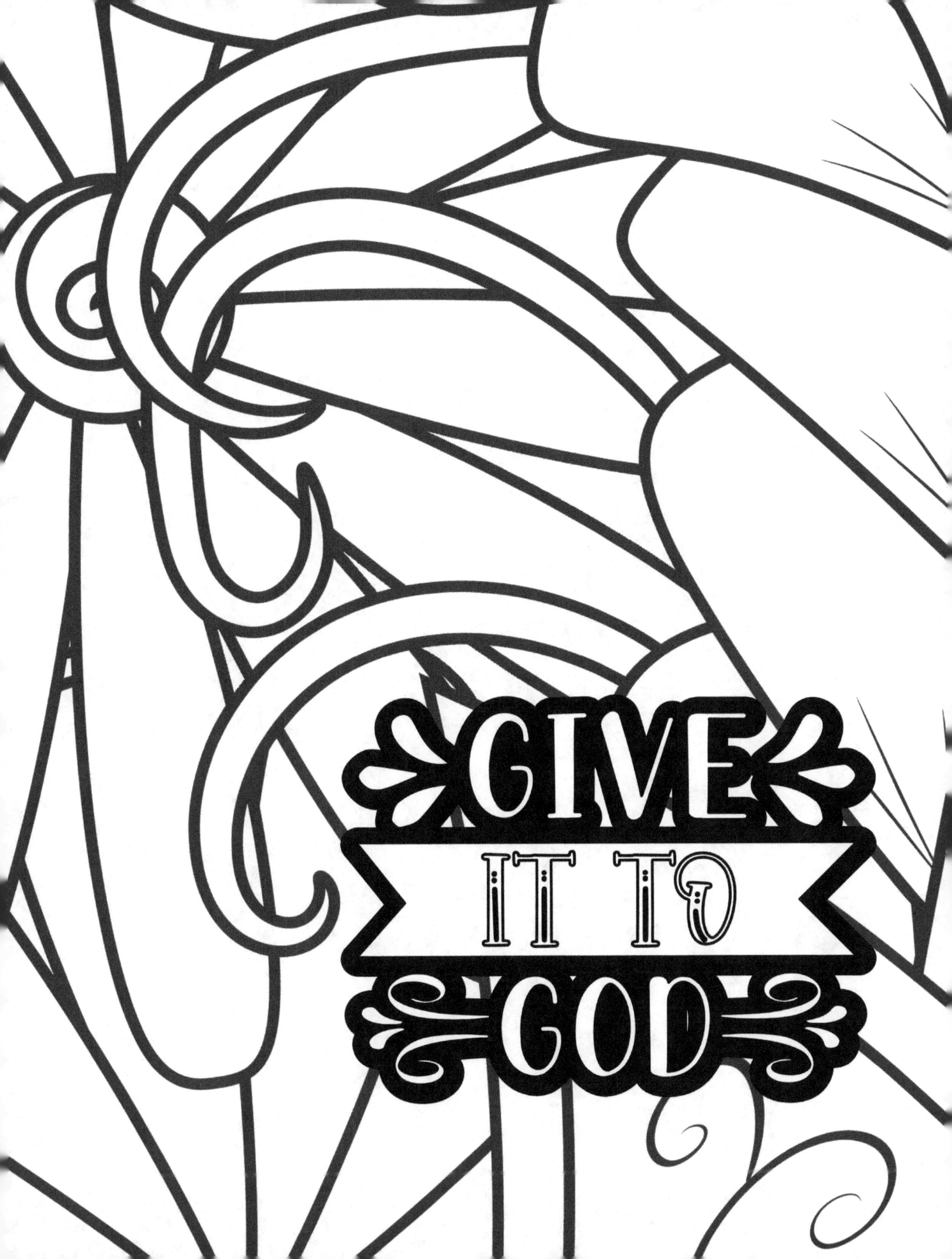
GIVE
IT TO
GOD

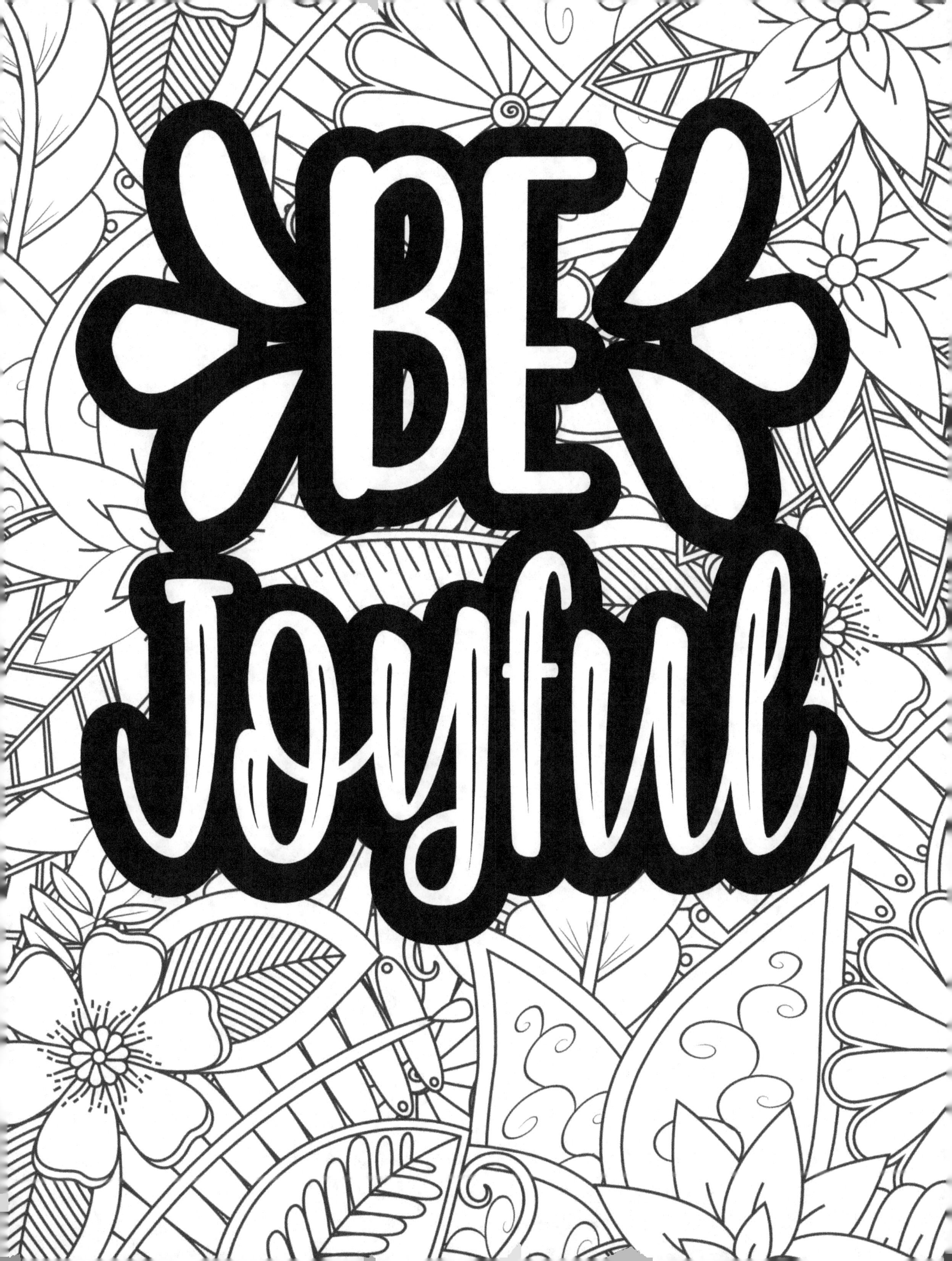
BE
Joyful

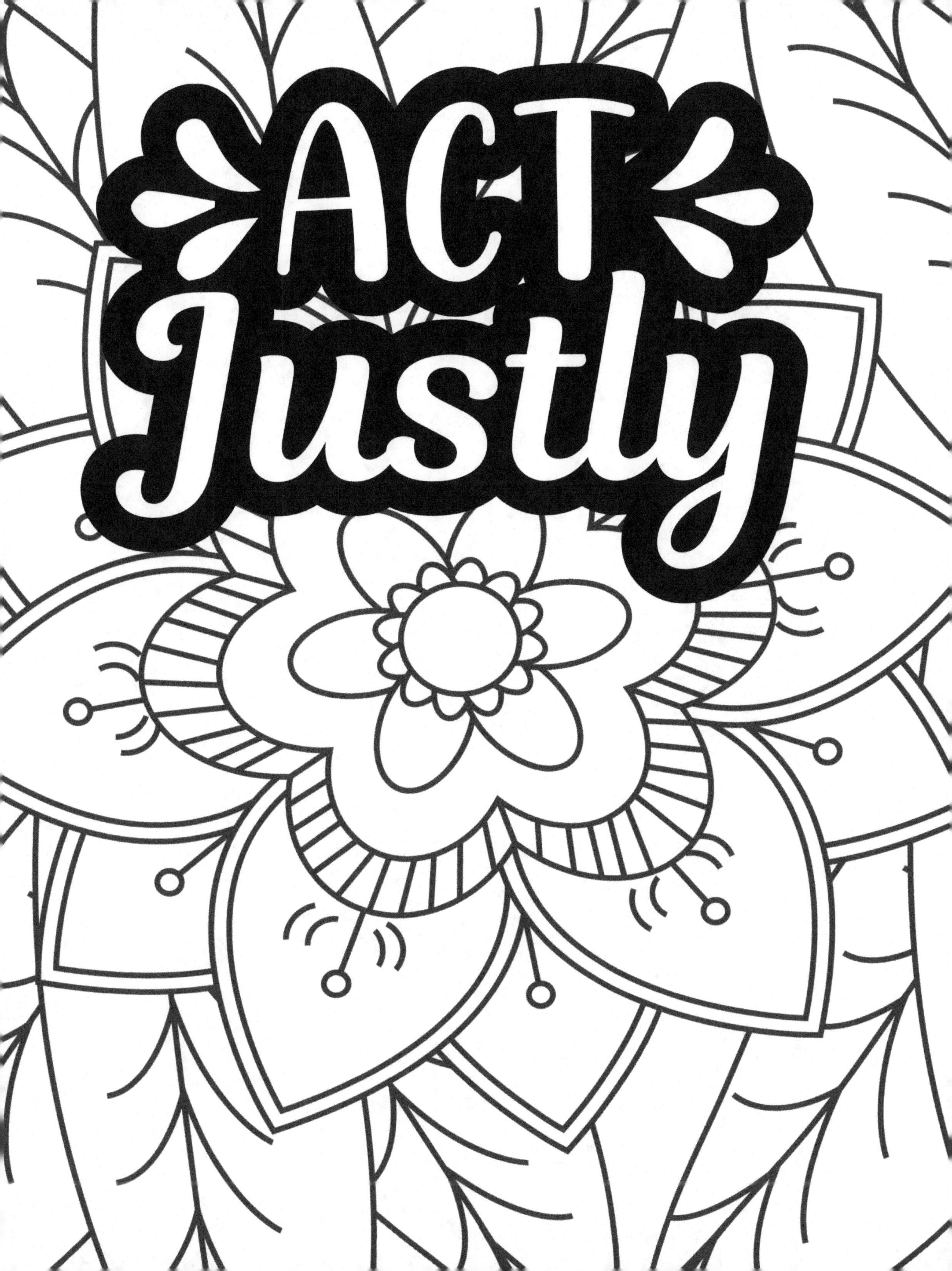
ACT
Justly

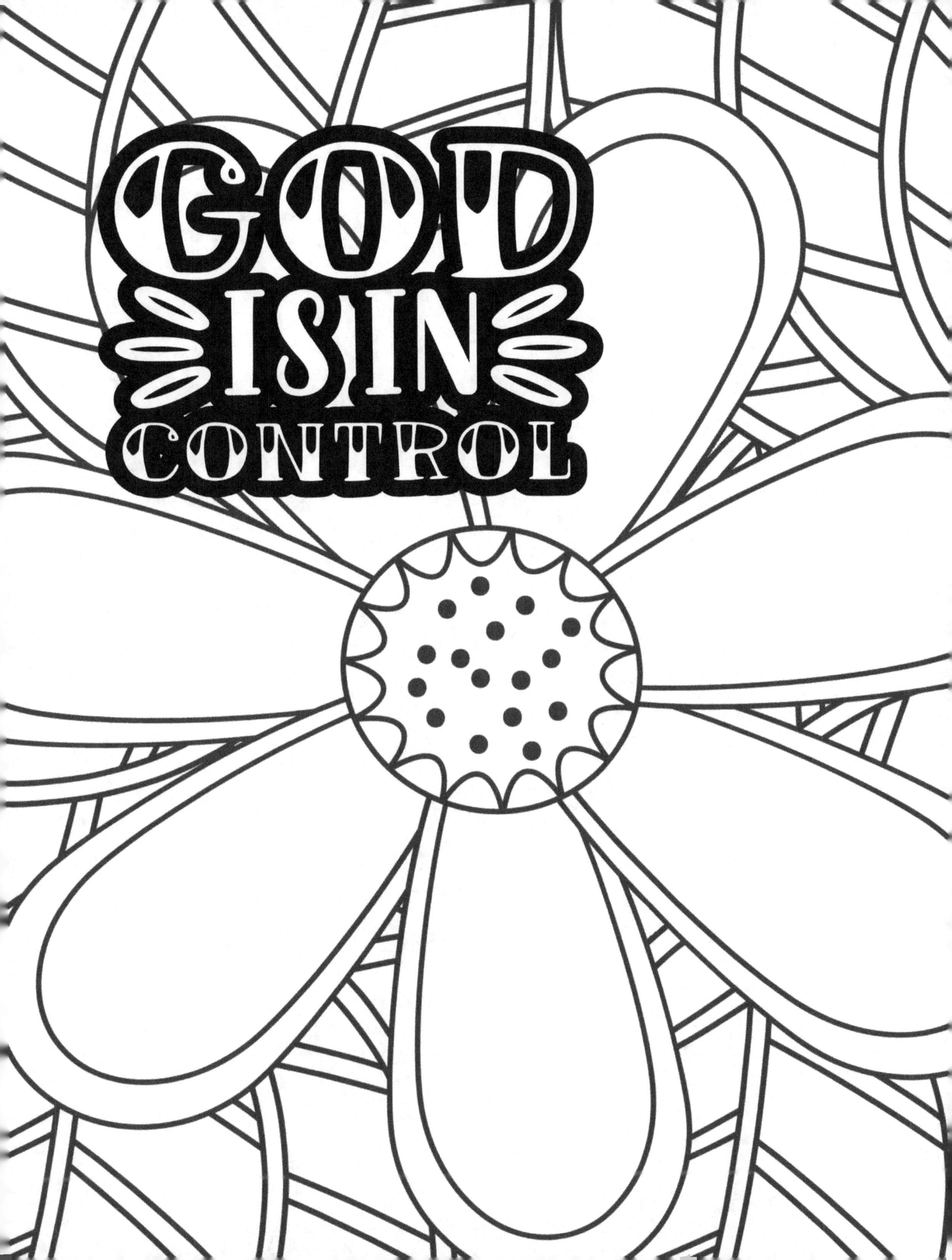
GOD
IS IN
CONTROL

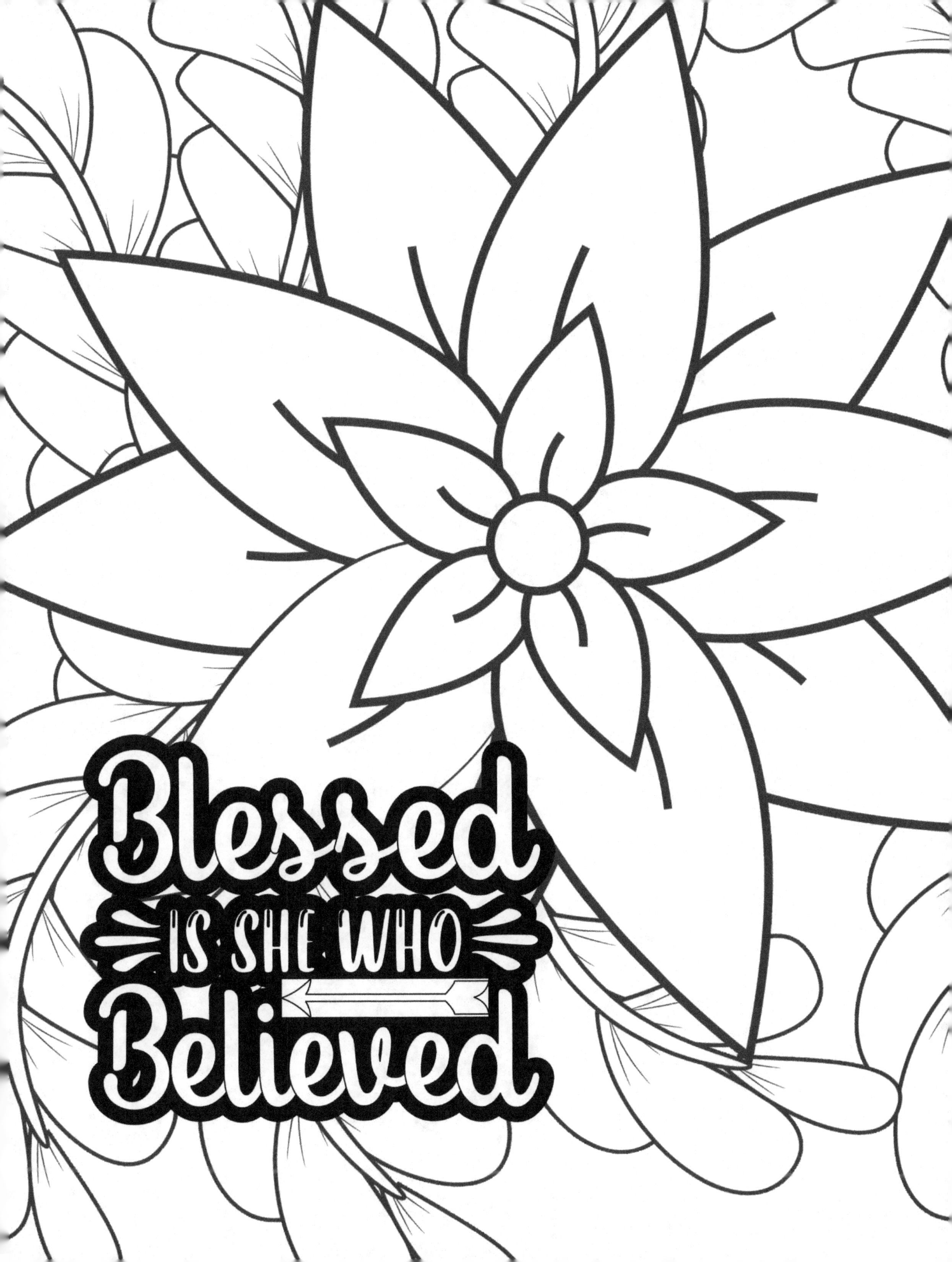
Blessed
IS SHE WHO
Believed

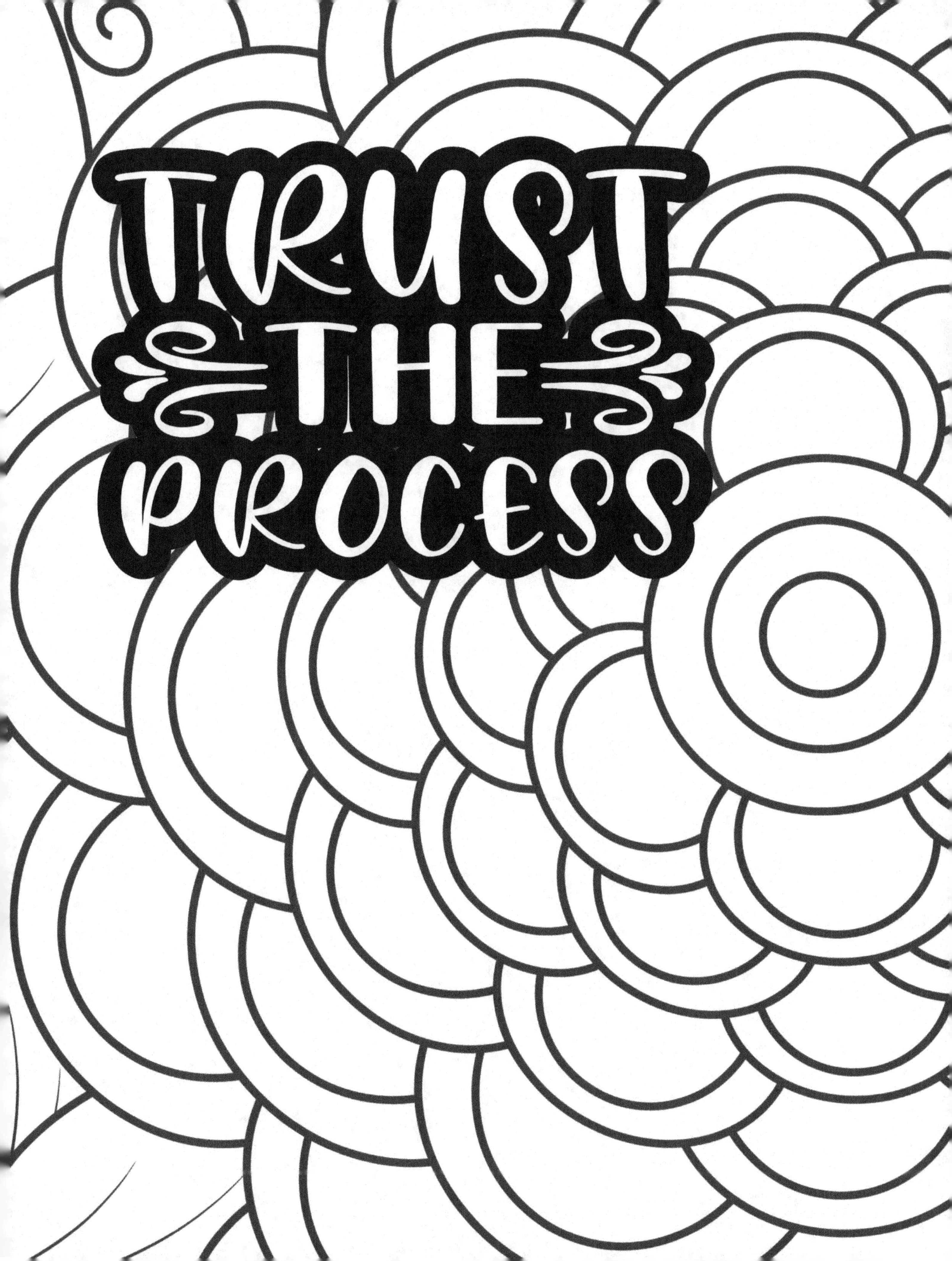
TRUST
THE
PROCESS

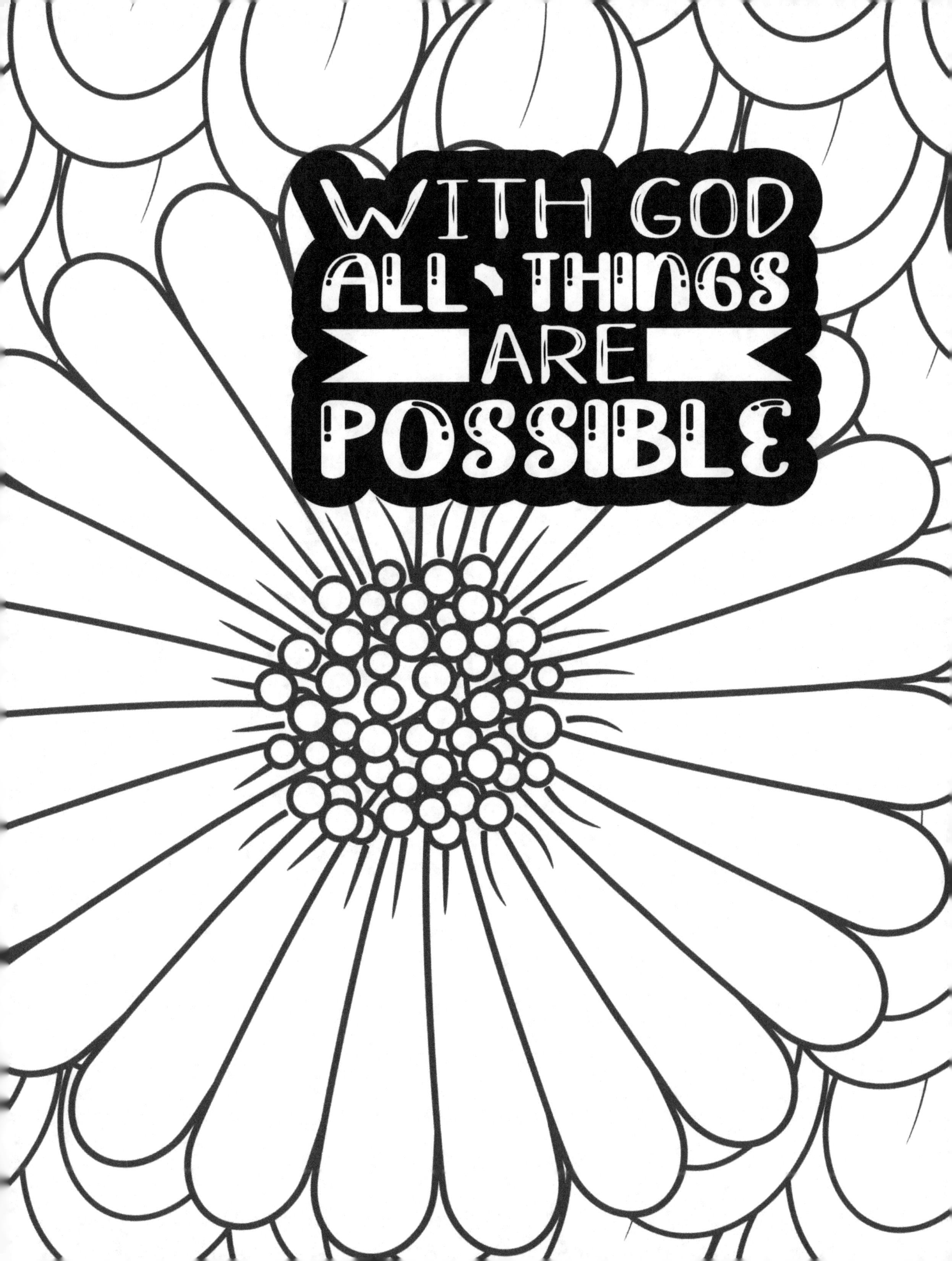
WITH GOD
ALL THINGS
ARE
POSSIBLE

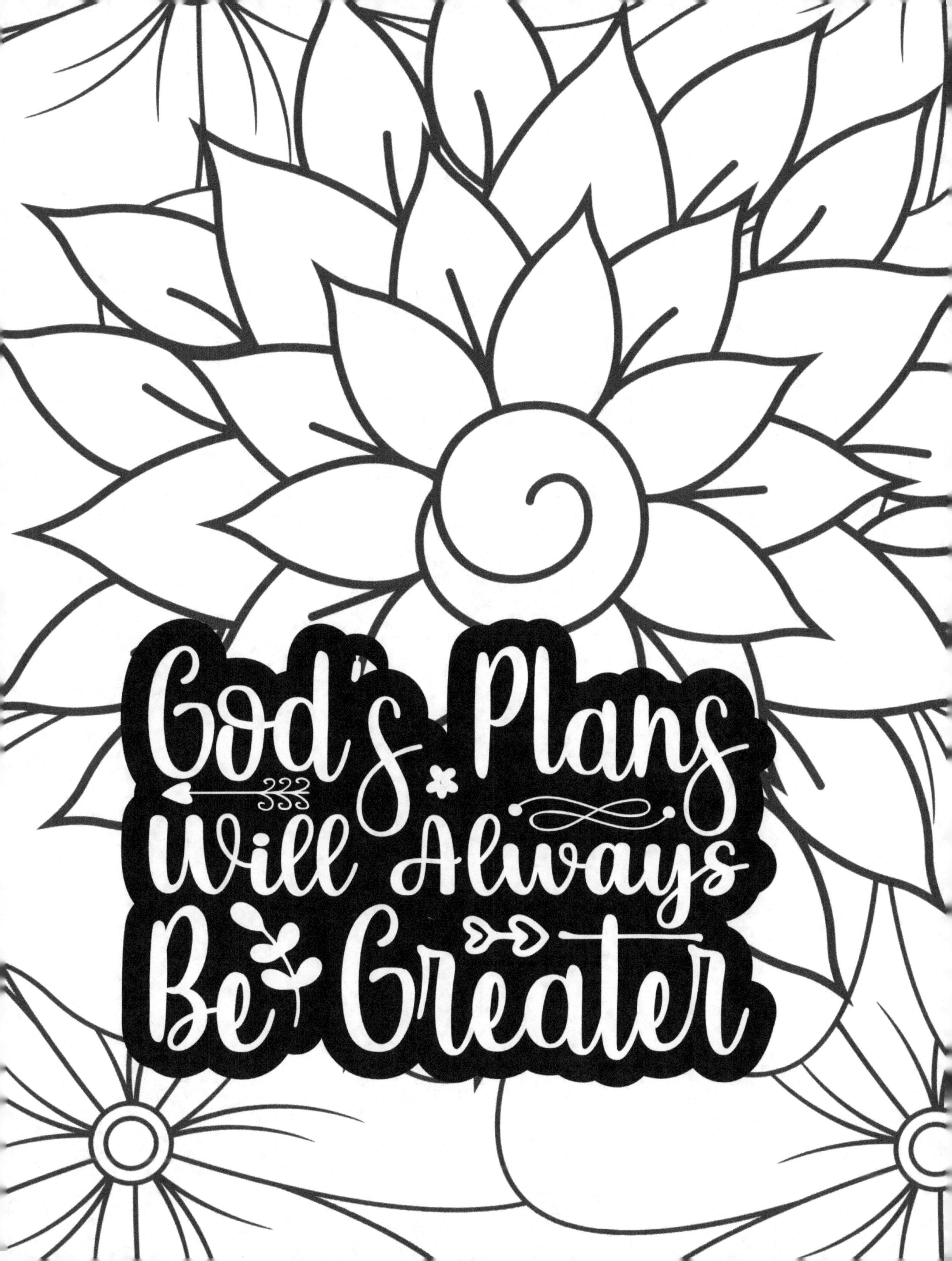
God's Plans
Will Always
Be Greater

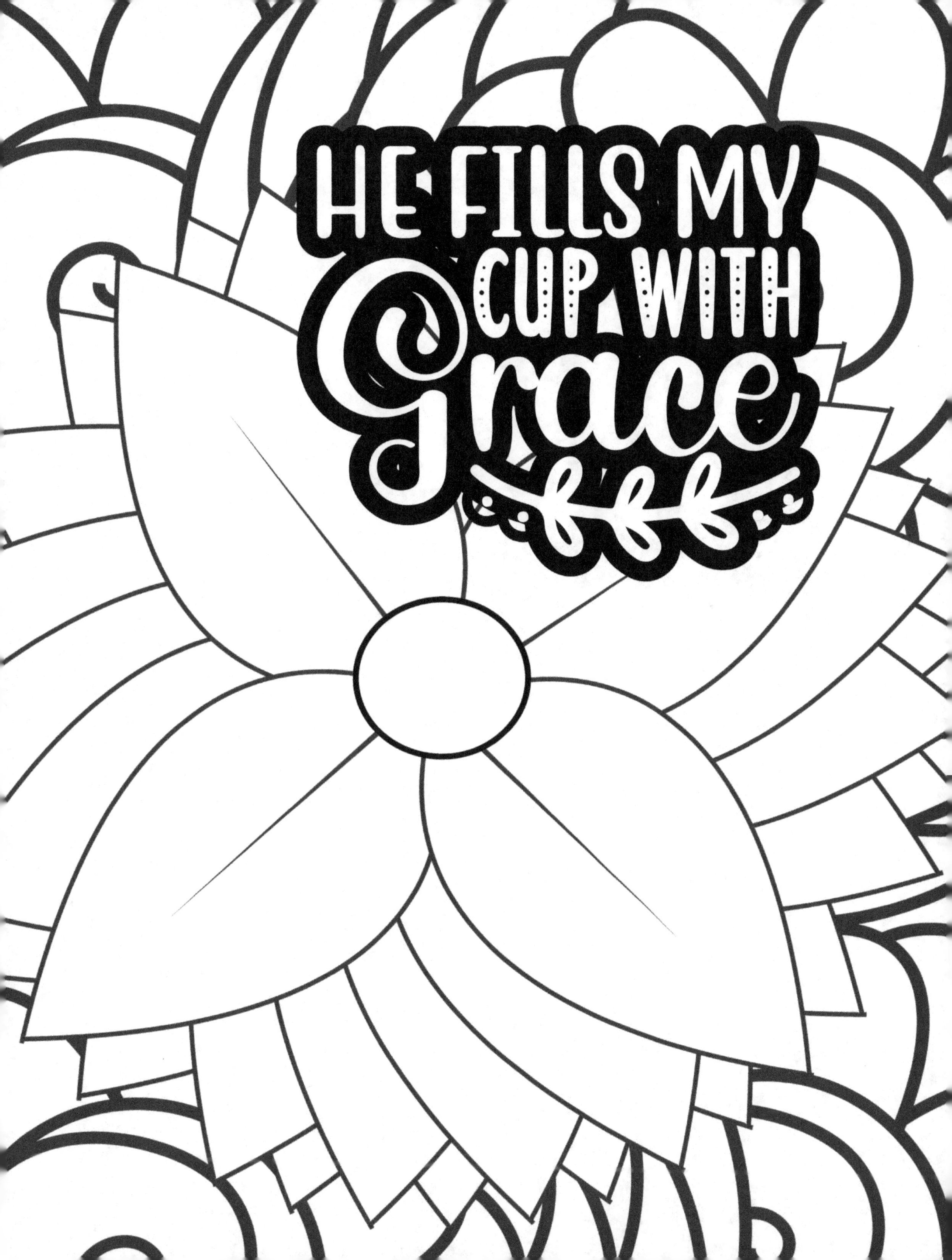
HE FILLS MY
CUP WITH
Grace

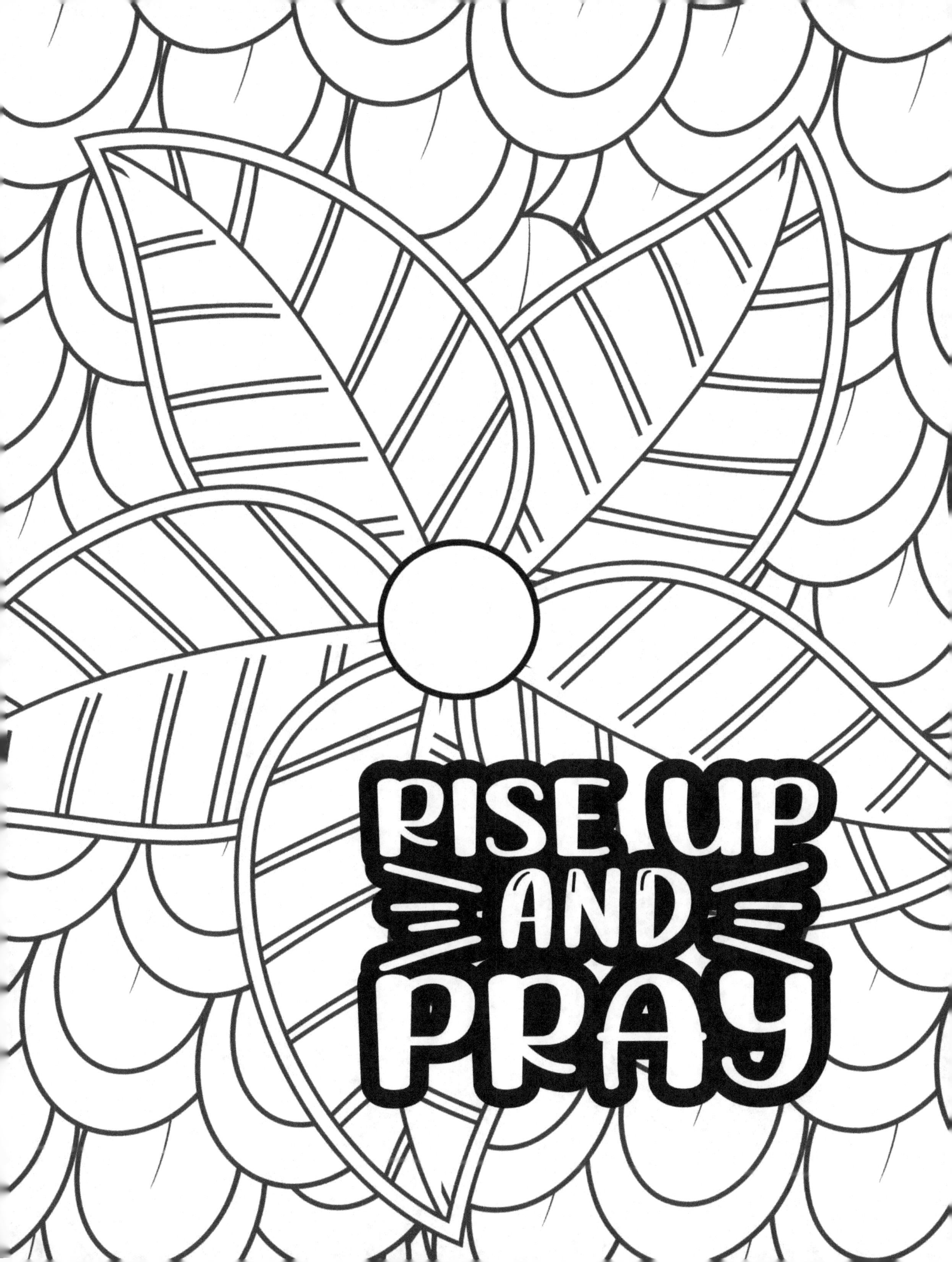
RISE UP
AND
PRAY

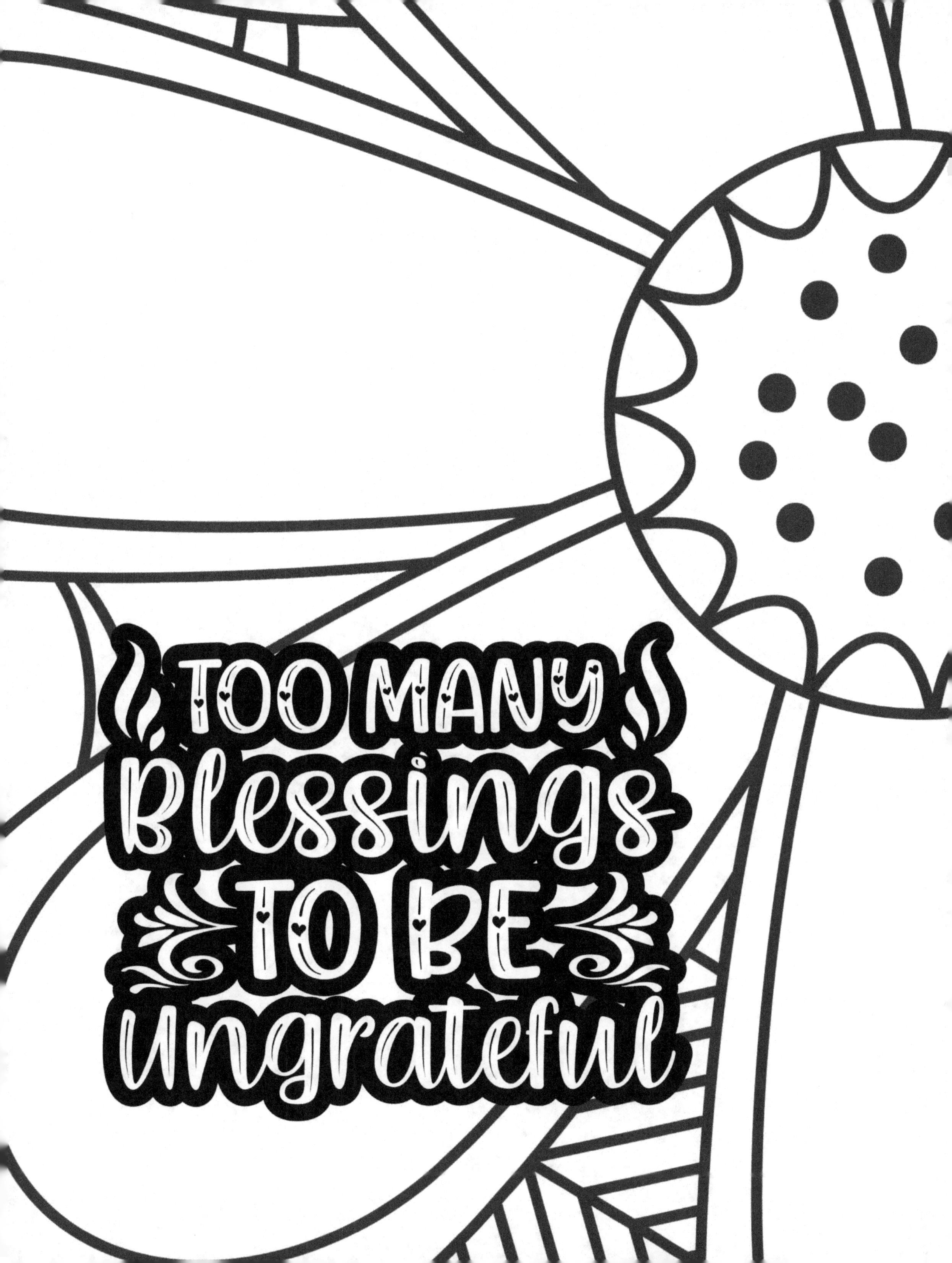
TOO MANY
Blessings
TO BE
Ungrateful

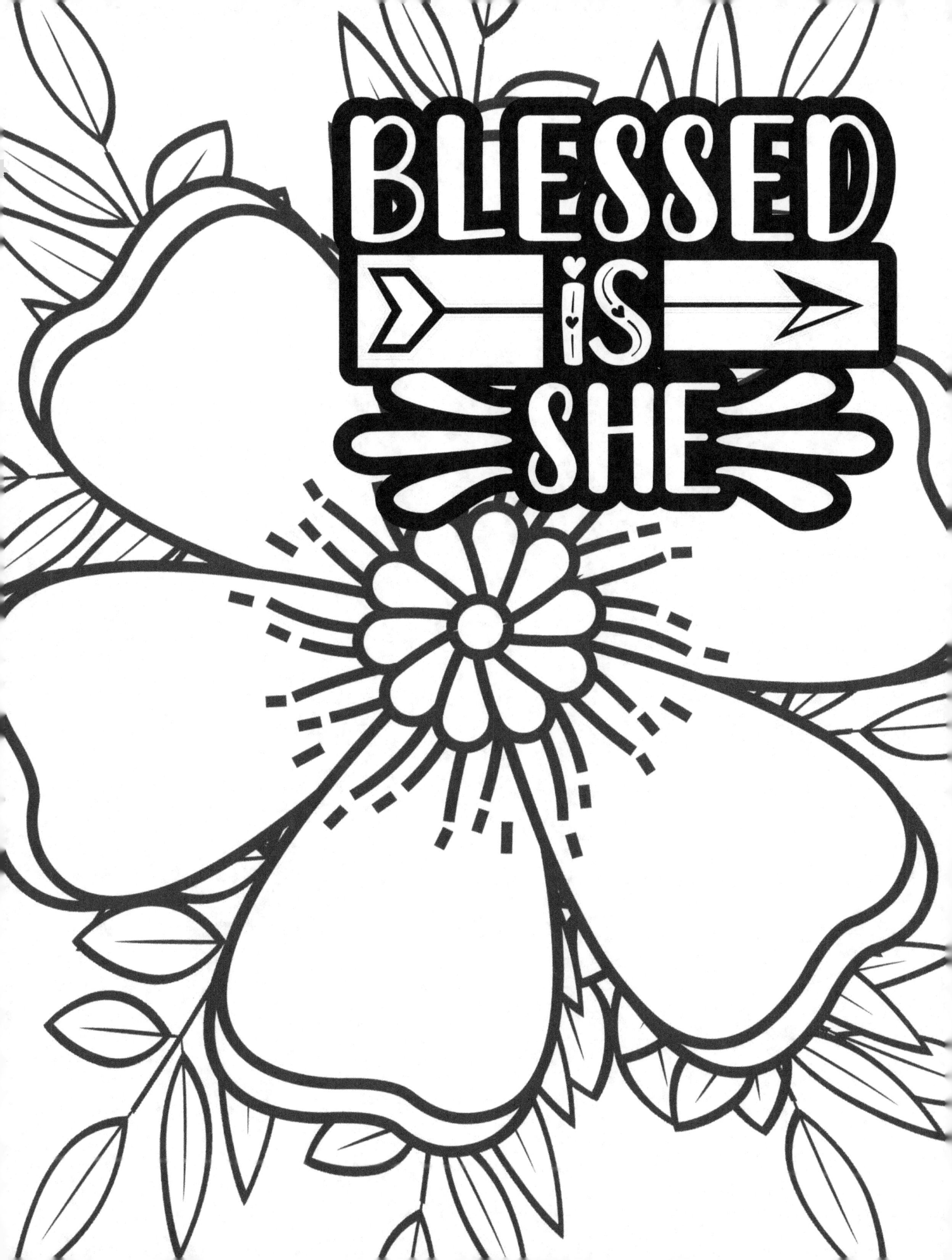
BLESSED
iS
SHE

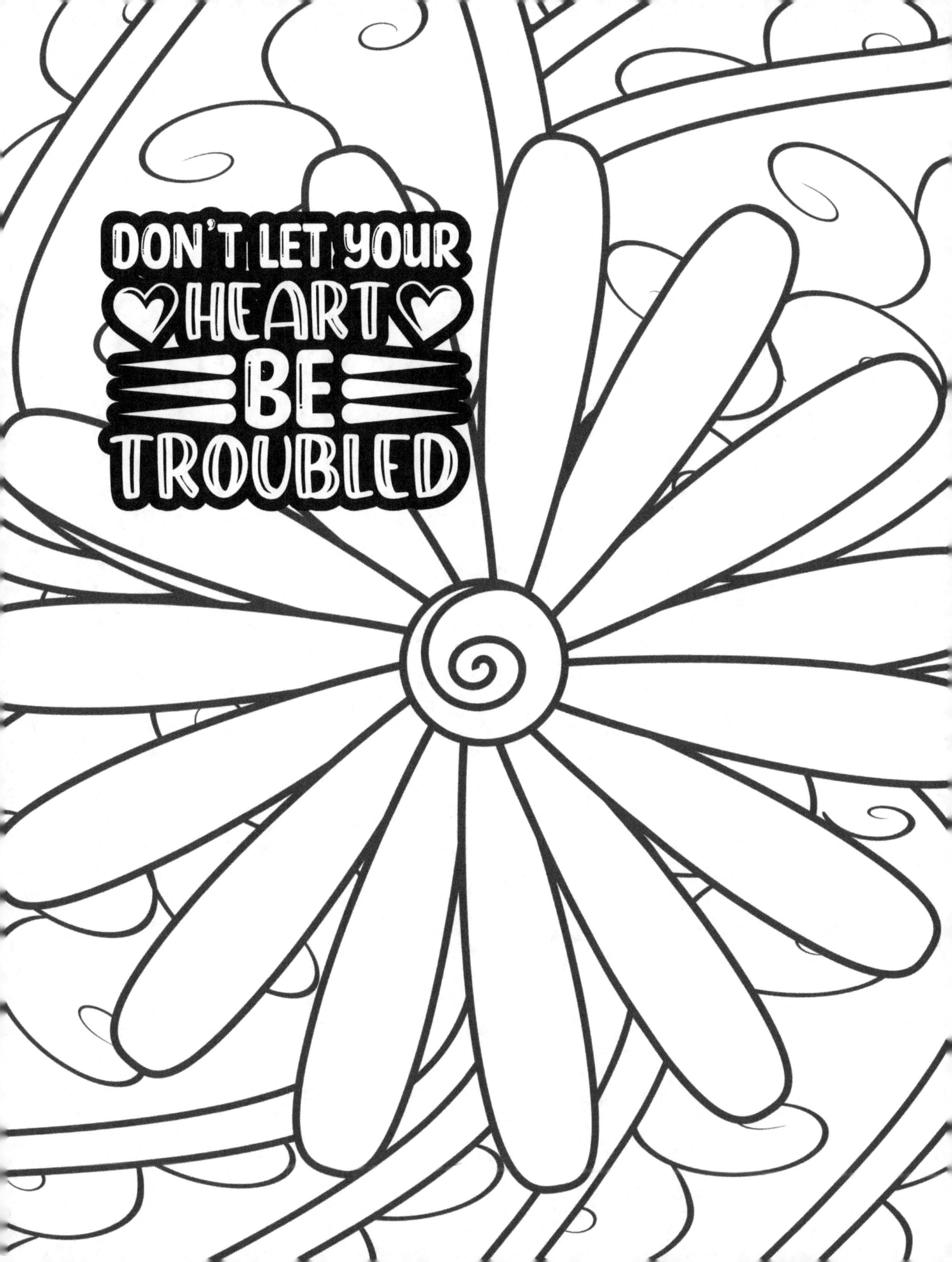
DON'T LET YOUR
HEART
BE
TROUBLED

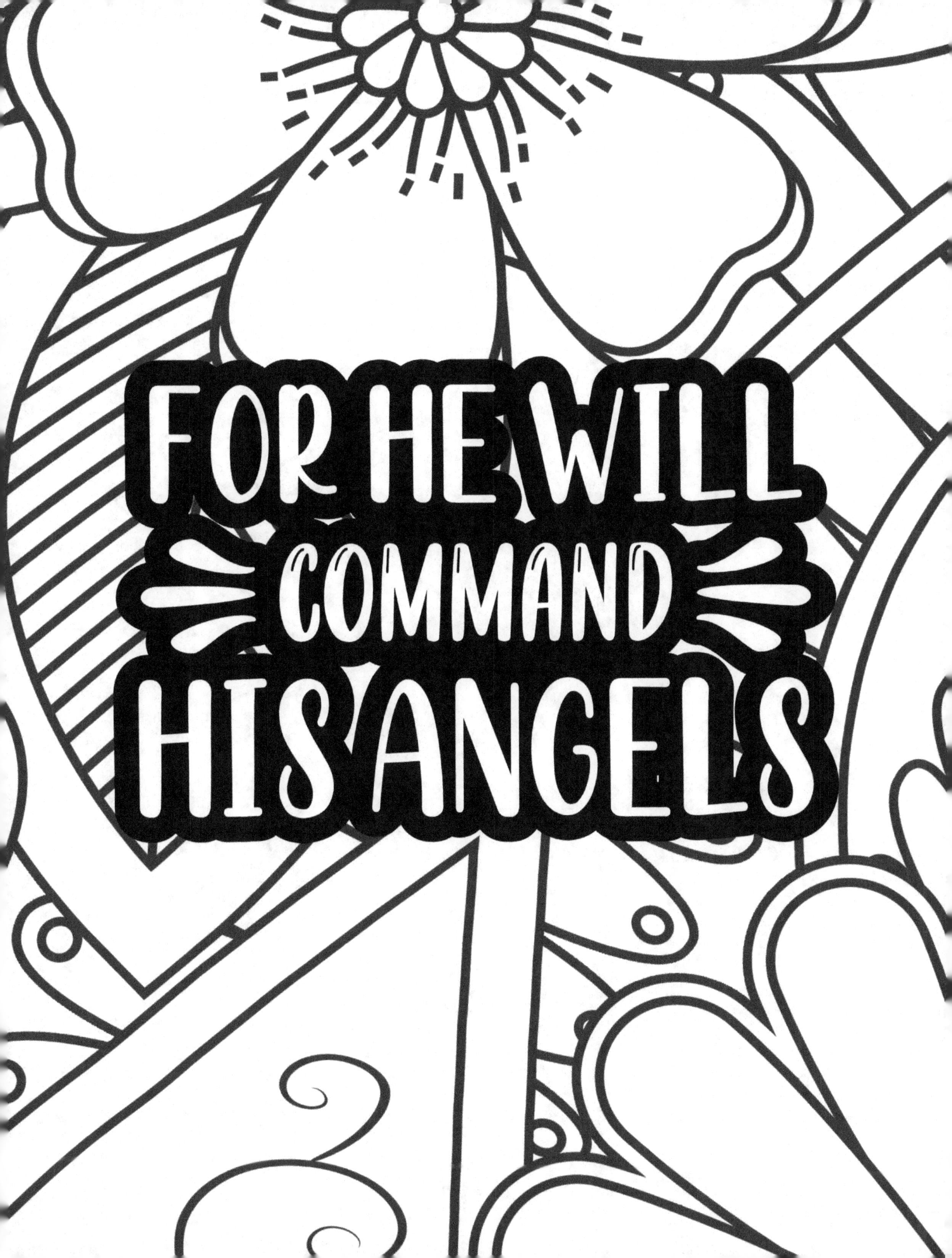
FOR HE WILL
COMMAND
HIS ANGELS

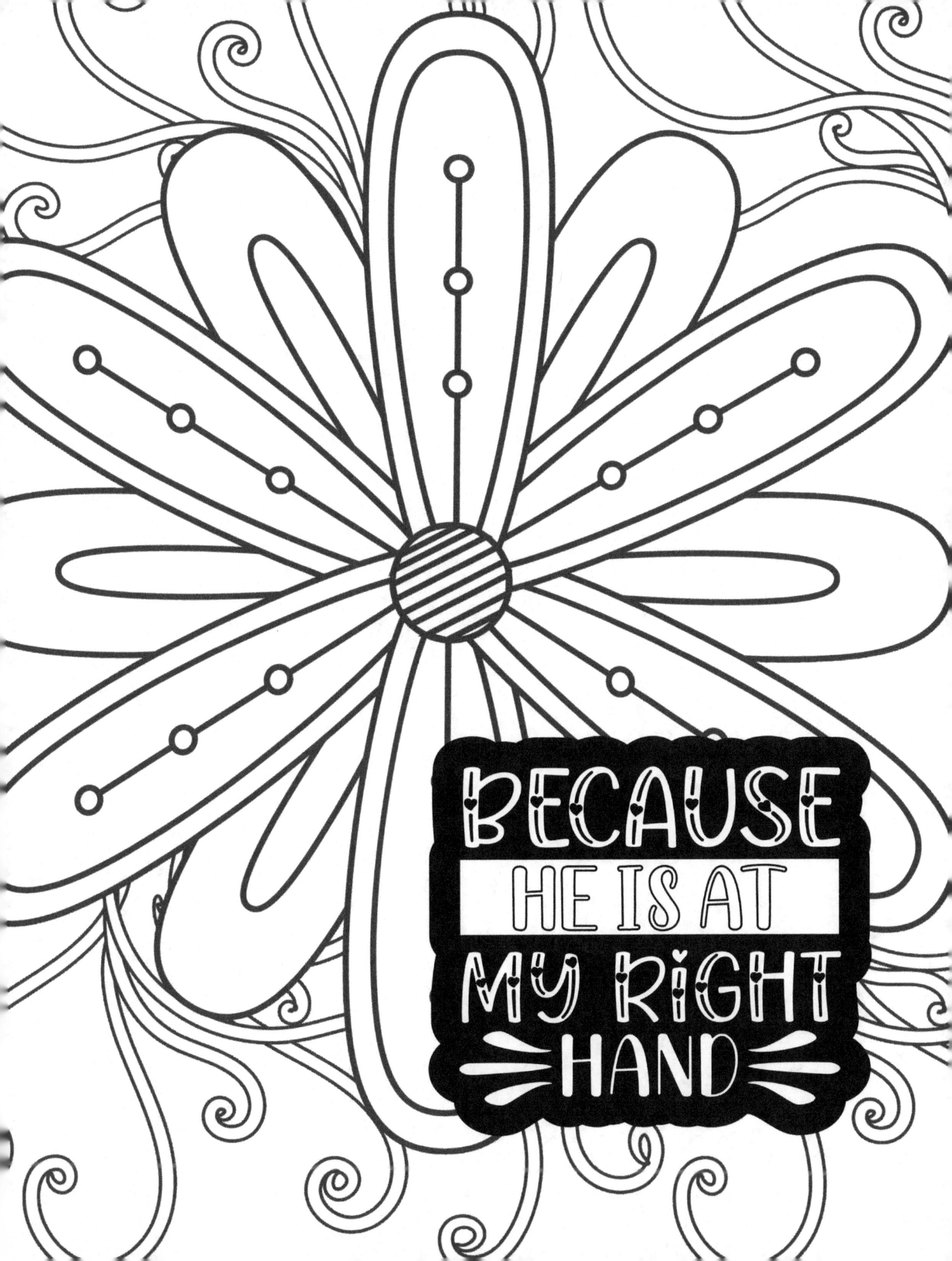
BECAUSE
HE IS AT
MY RIGHT
HAND

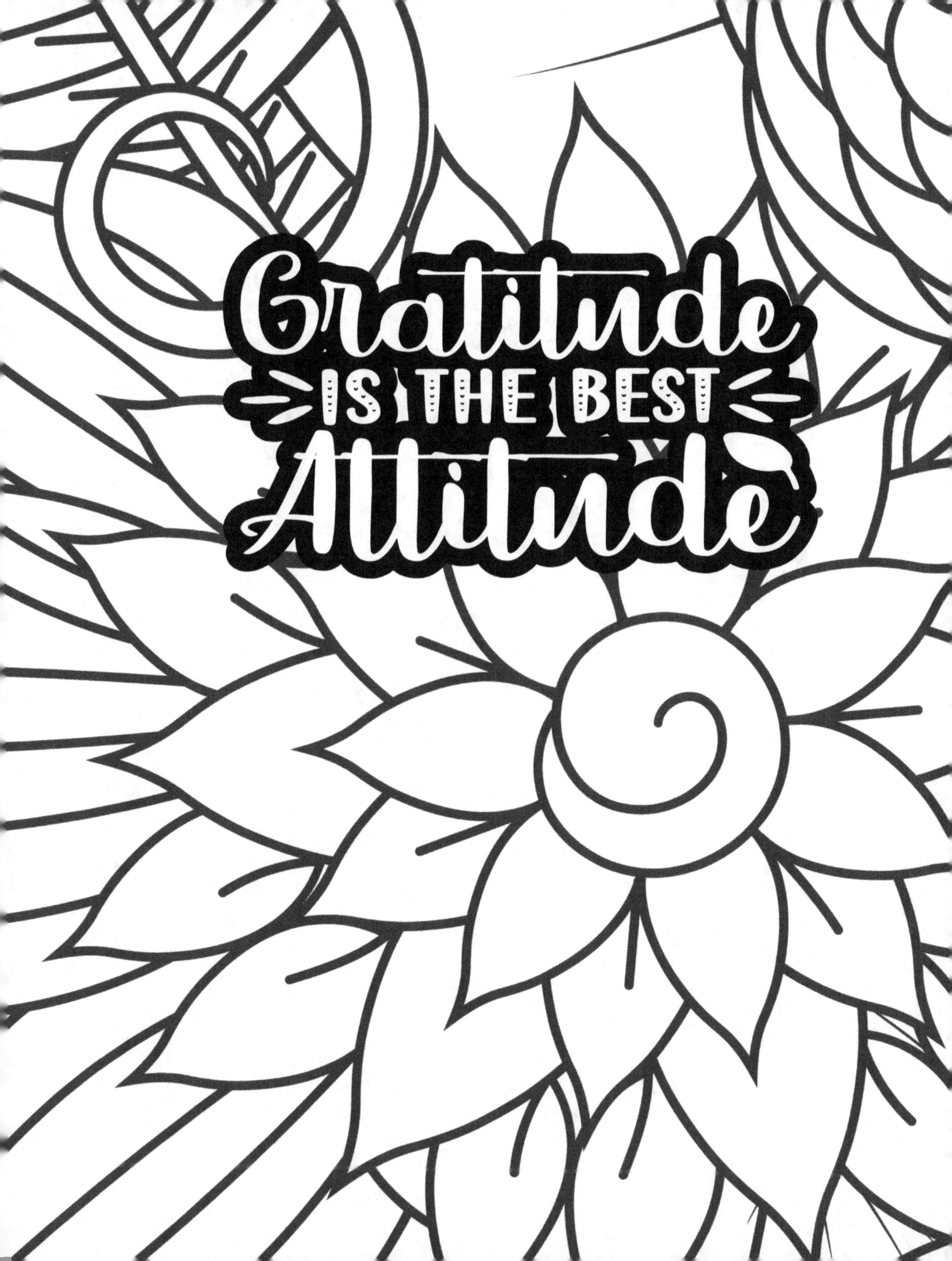
Gratitude
IS THE BEST
Attitude

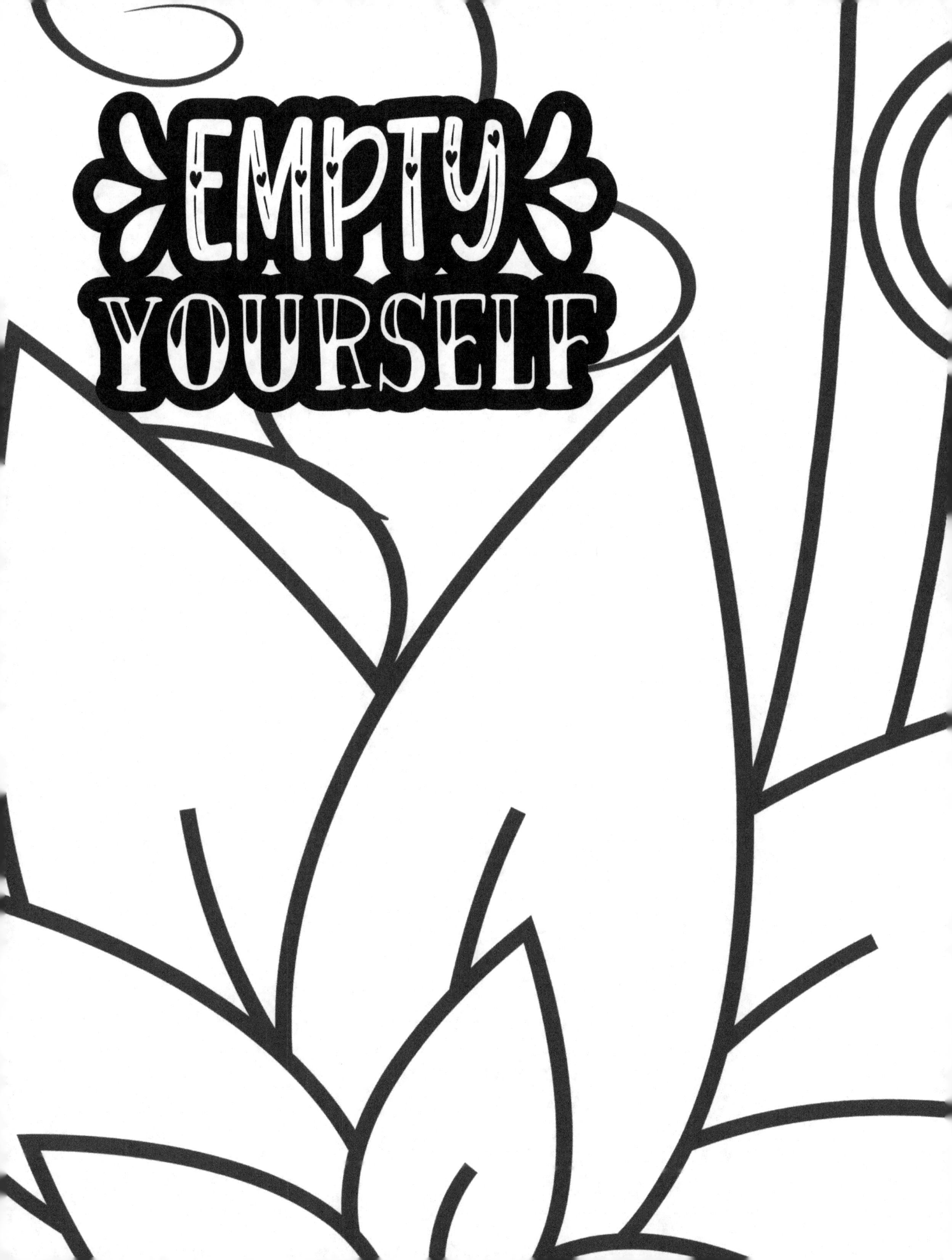
EMPTY
YOURSELF

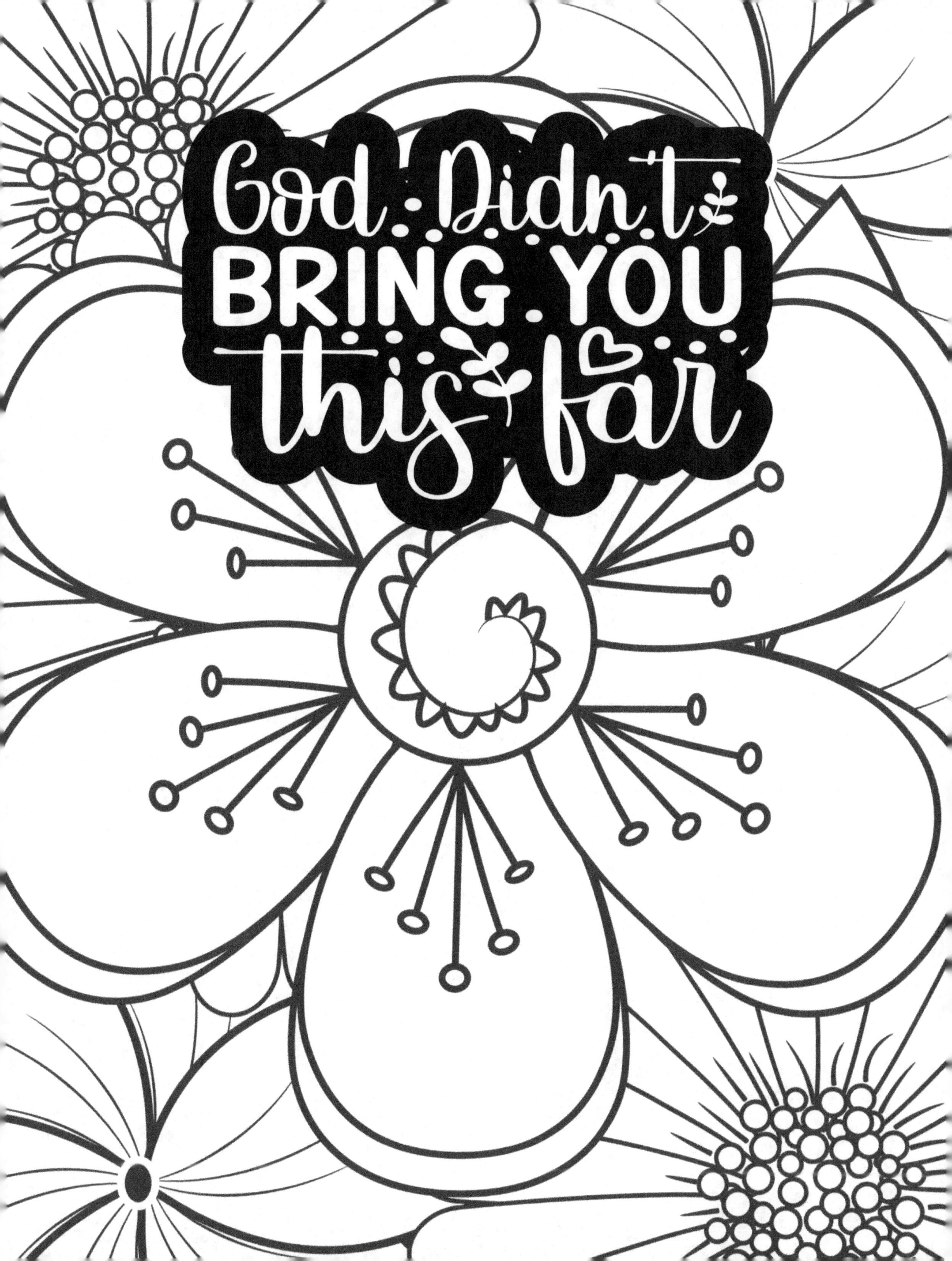
God Didn't
BRING YOU
this far

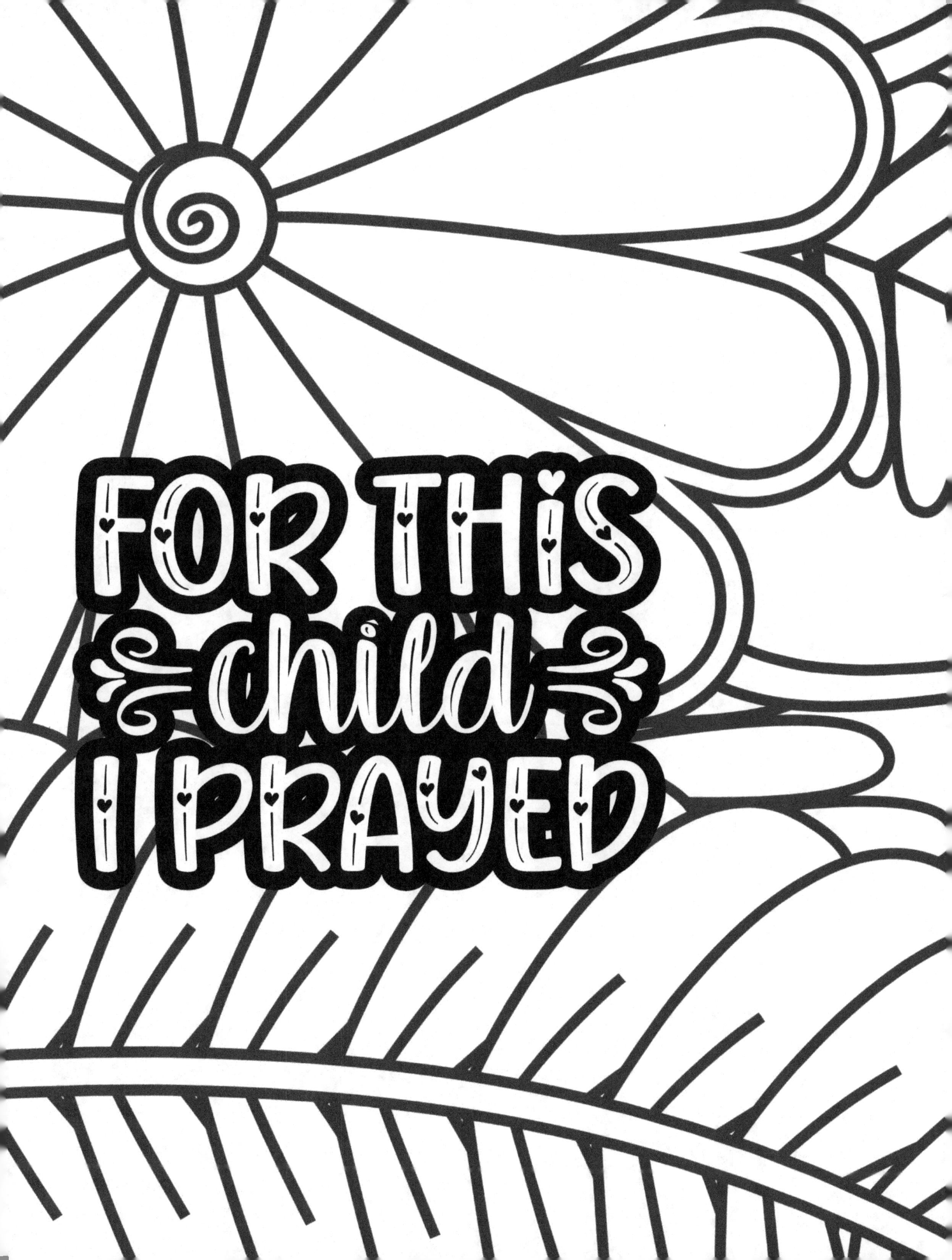
FOR THIS
child
I PRAYED

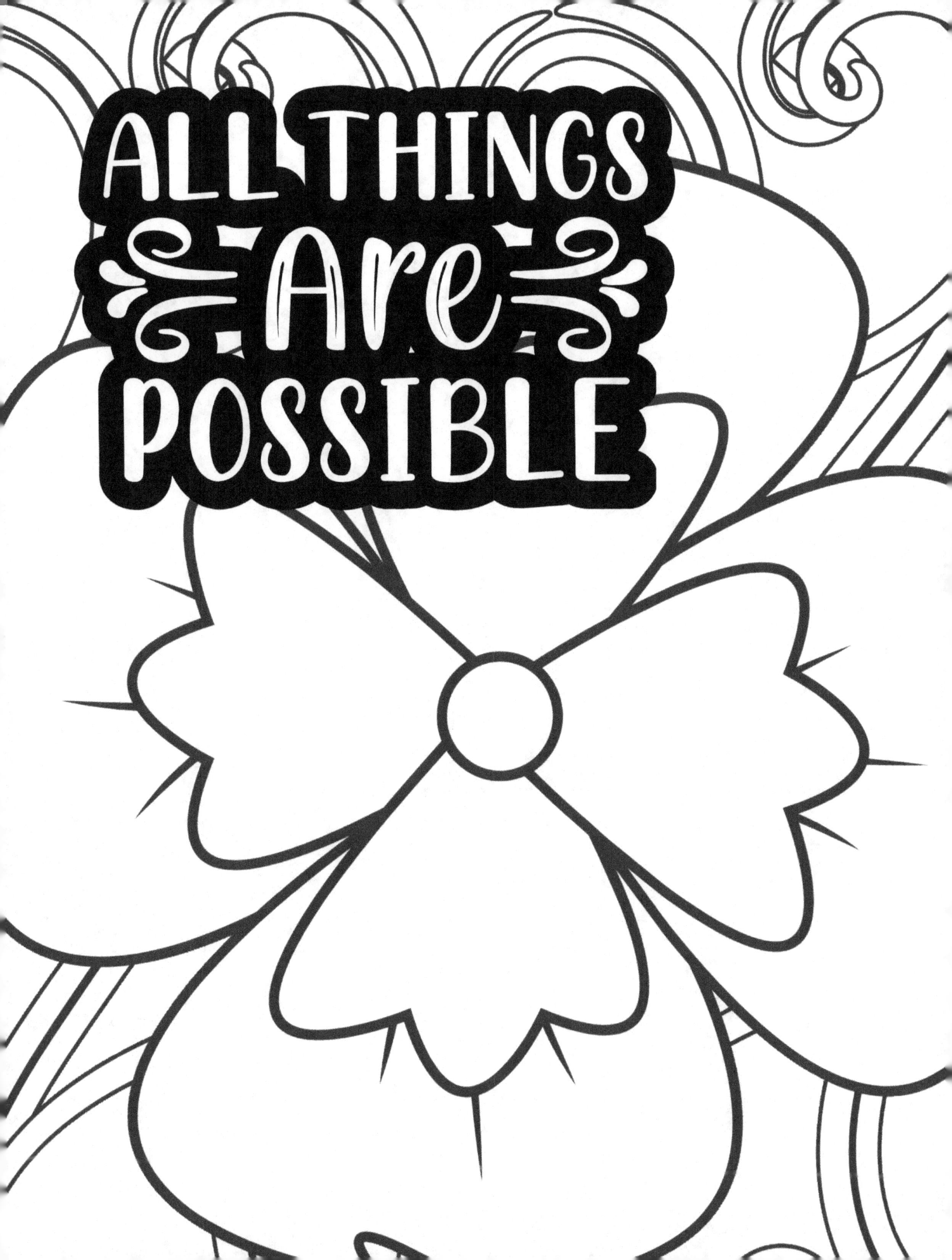
ALL THINGS
Are
POSSIBLE

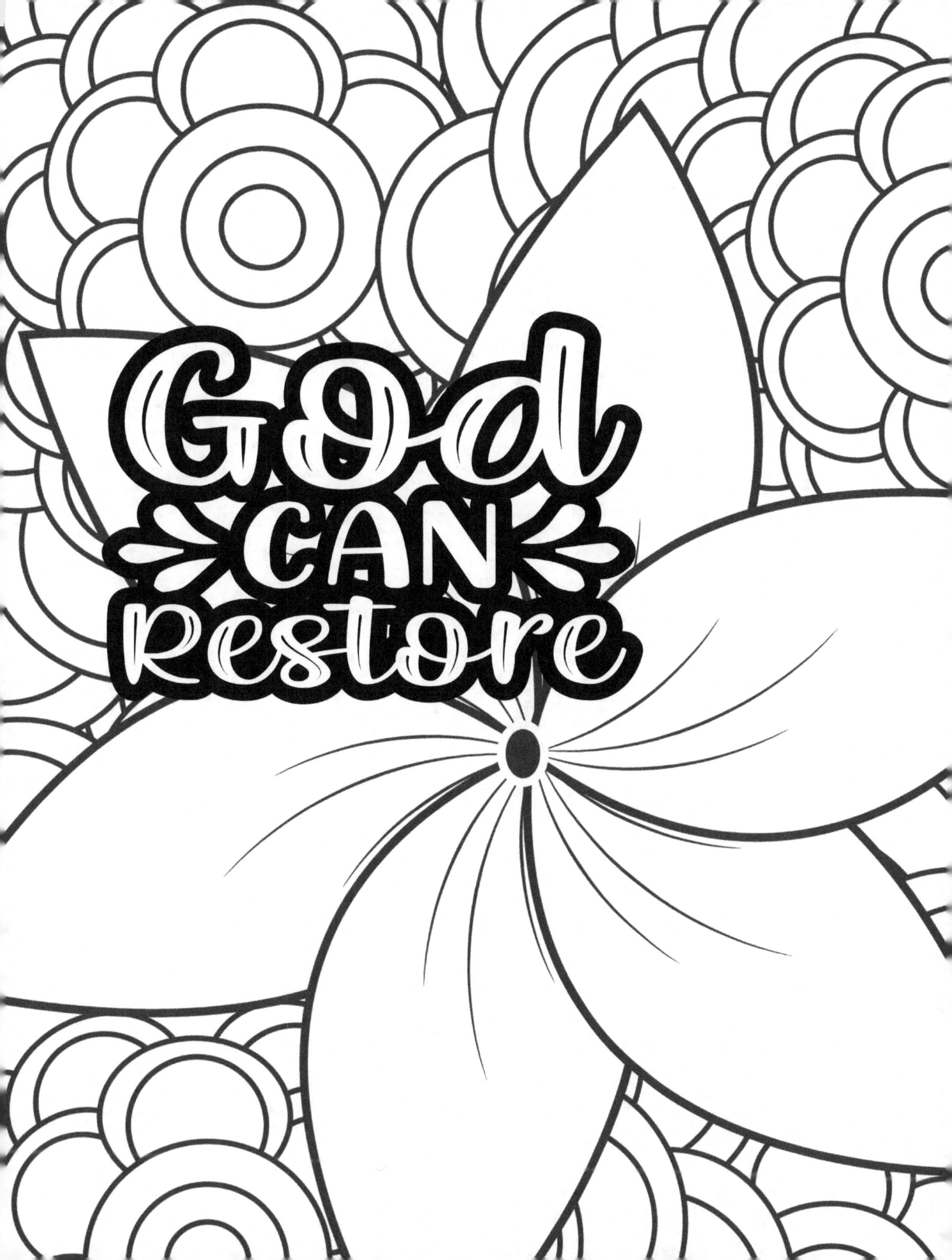
God
CAN
Restore

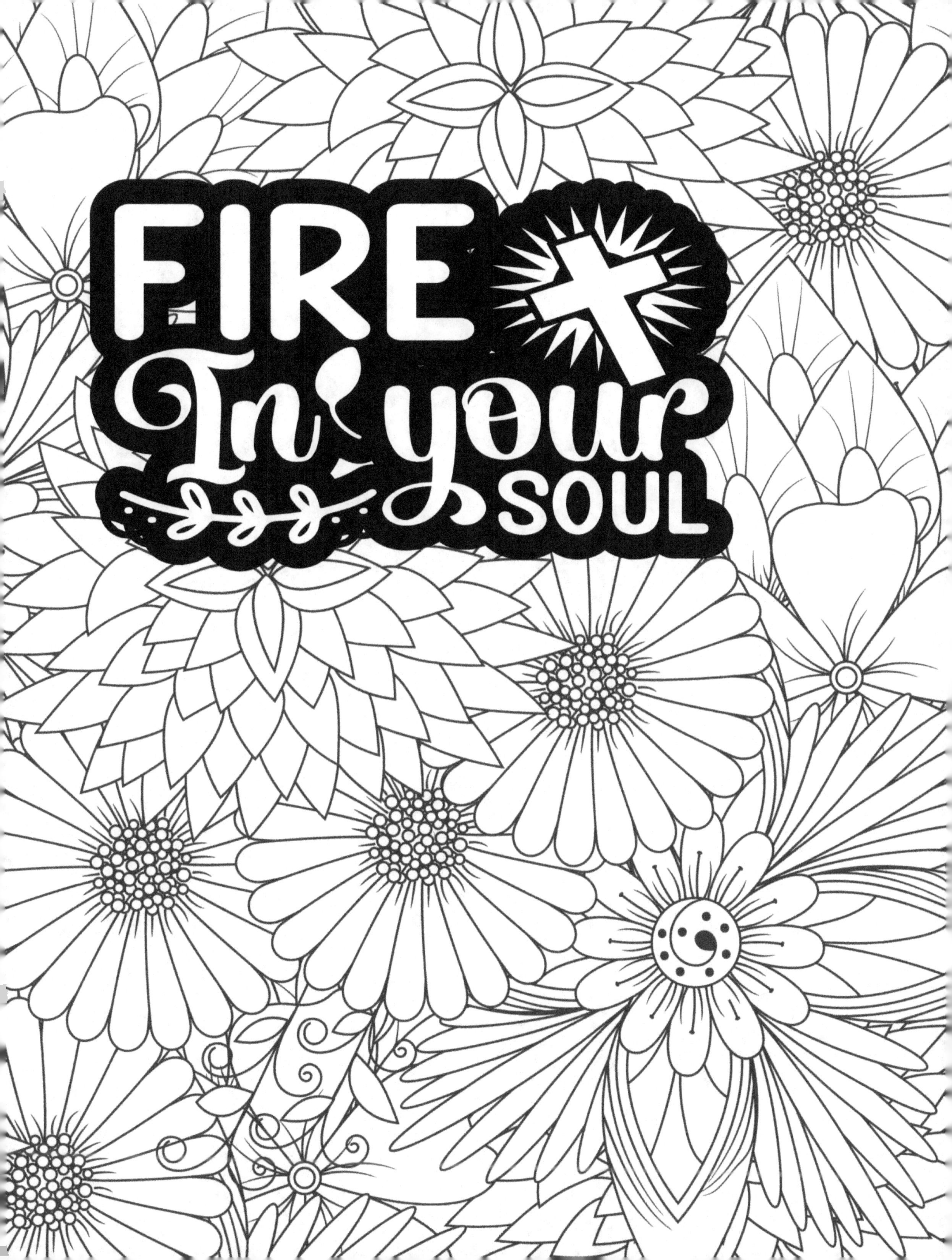
FIRE
In your
SOUL

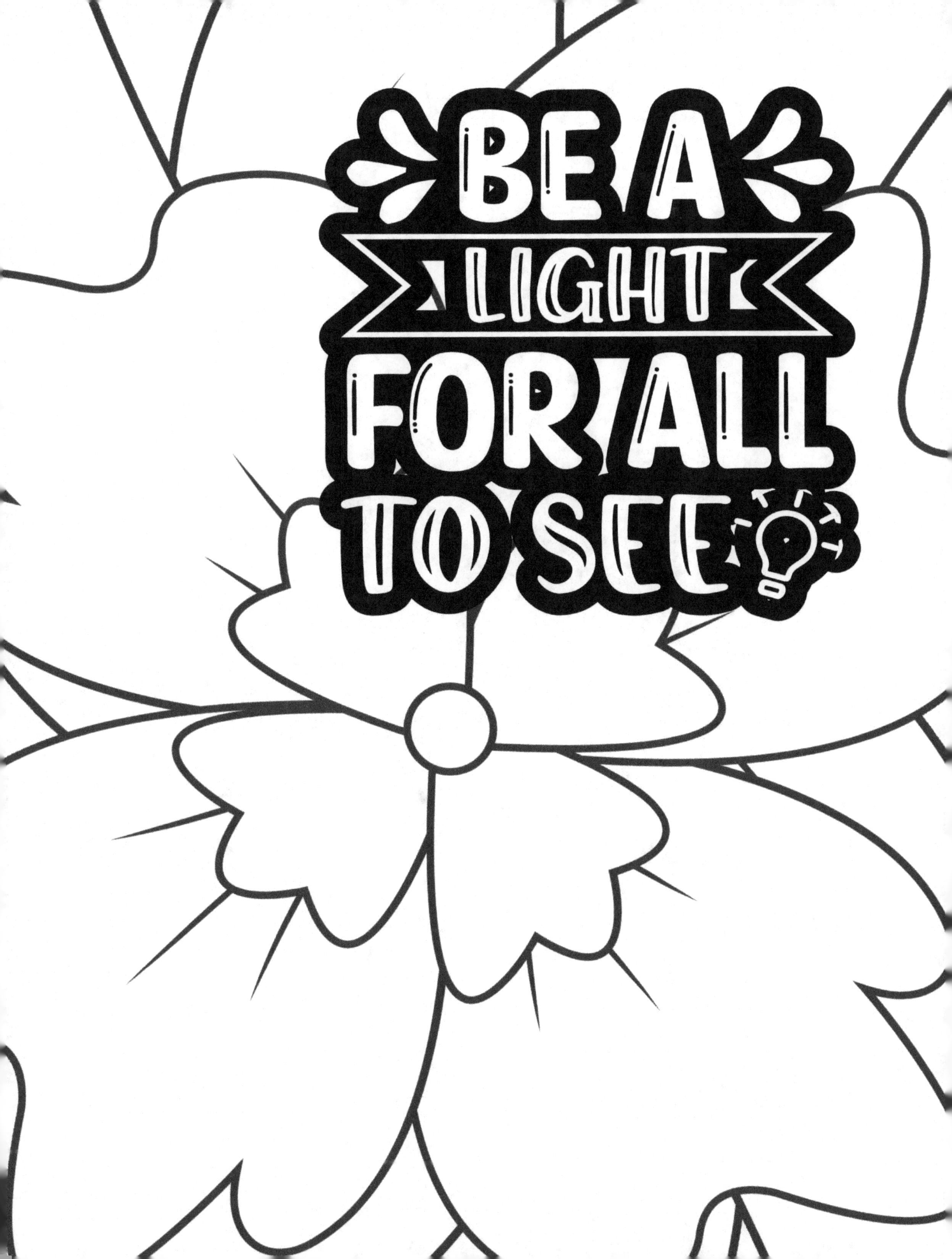
BE A
LIGHT
FOR ALL
TO SEE

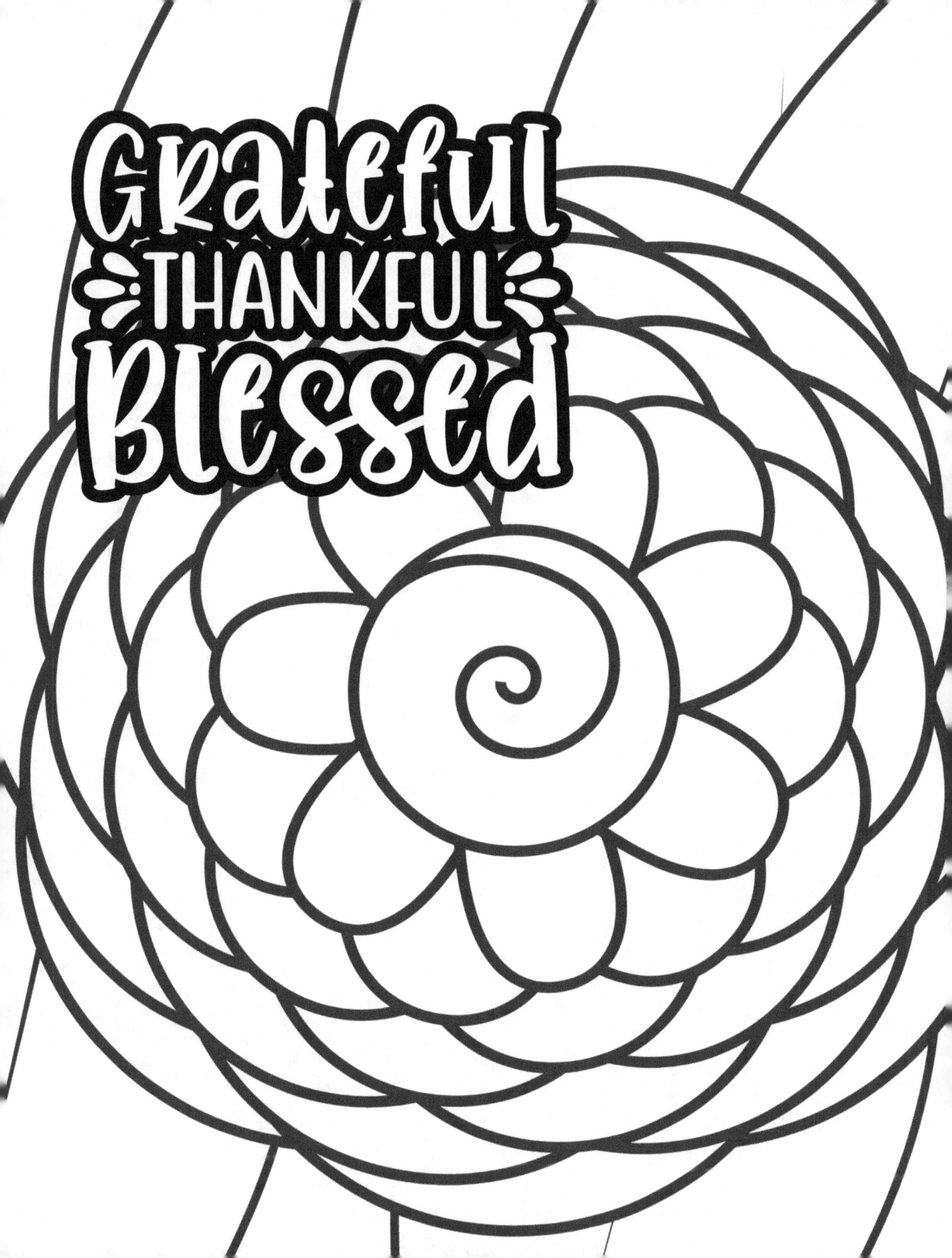
Grateful
THANKFUL
Blessed

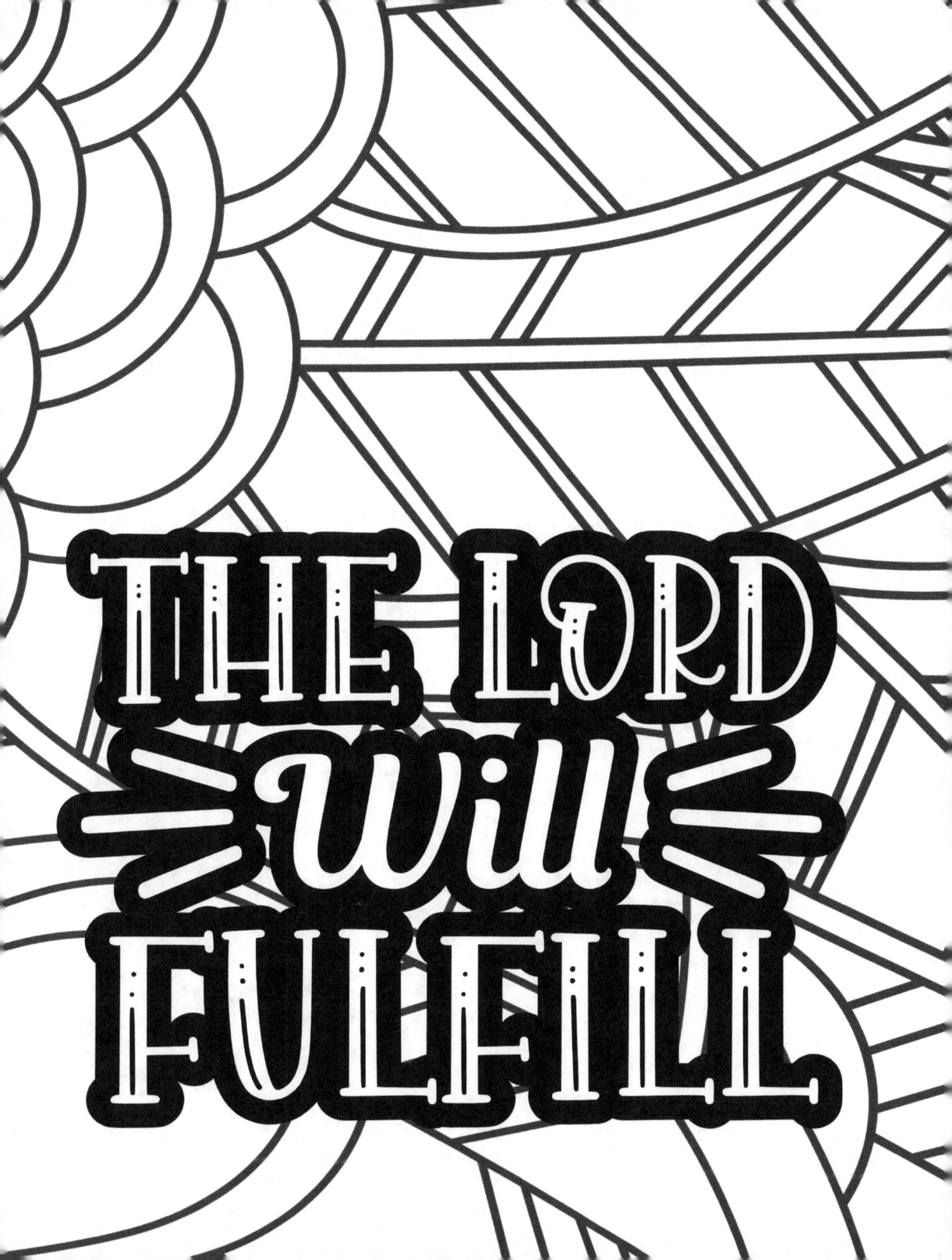
THE LORD
Will
FULFILL

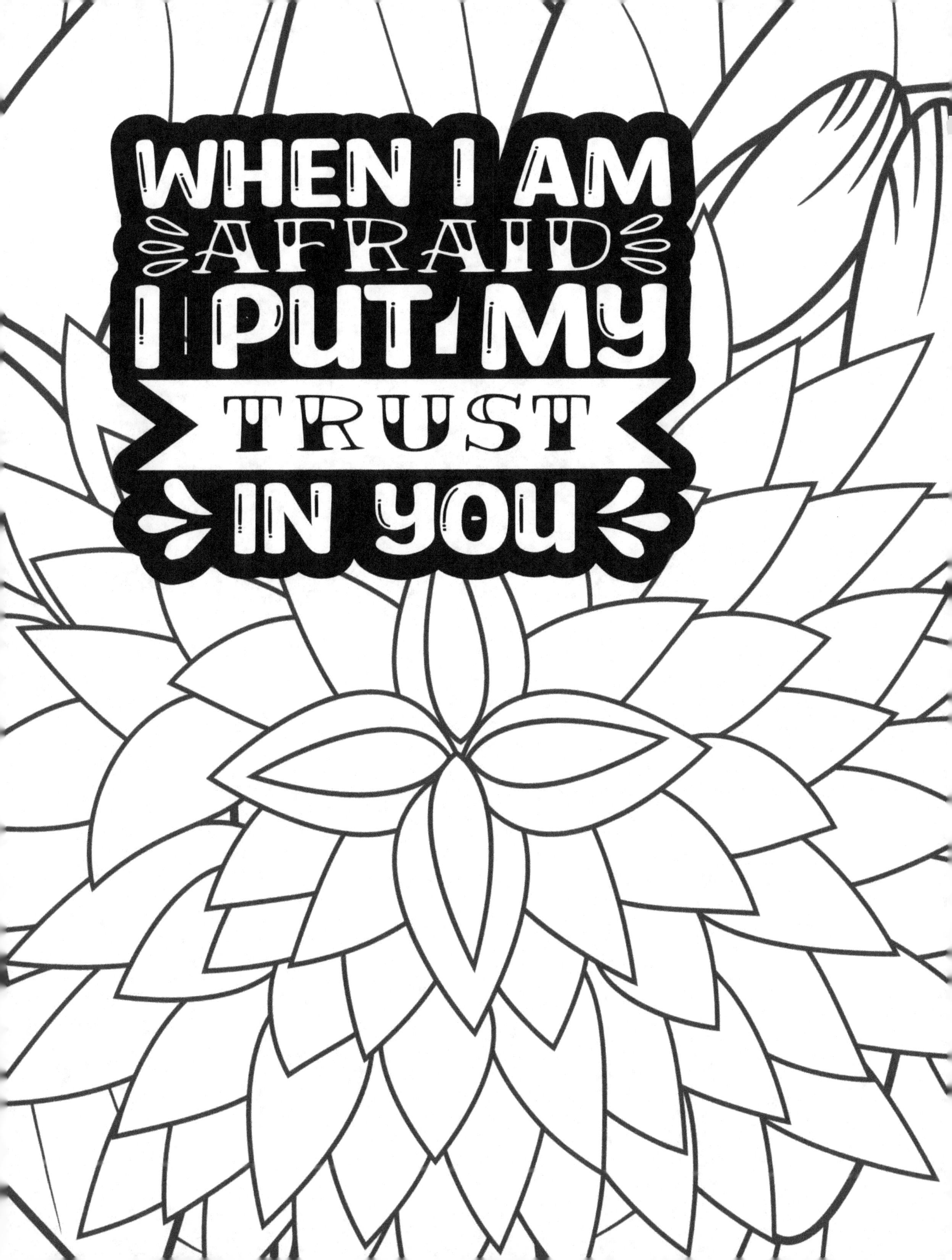
WHEN I AM
AFRAID
I PUT MY
TRUST
IN YOU

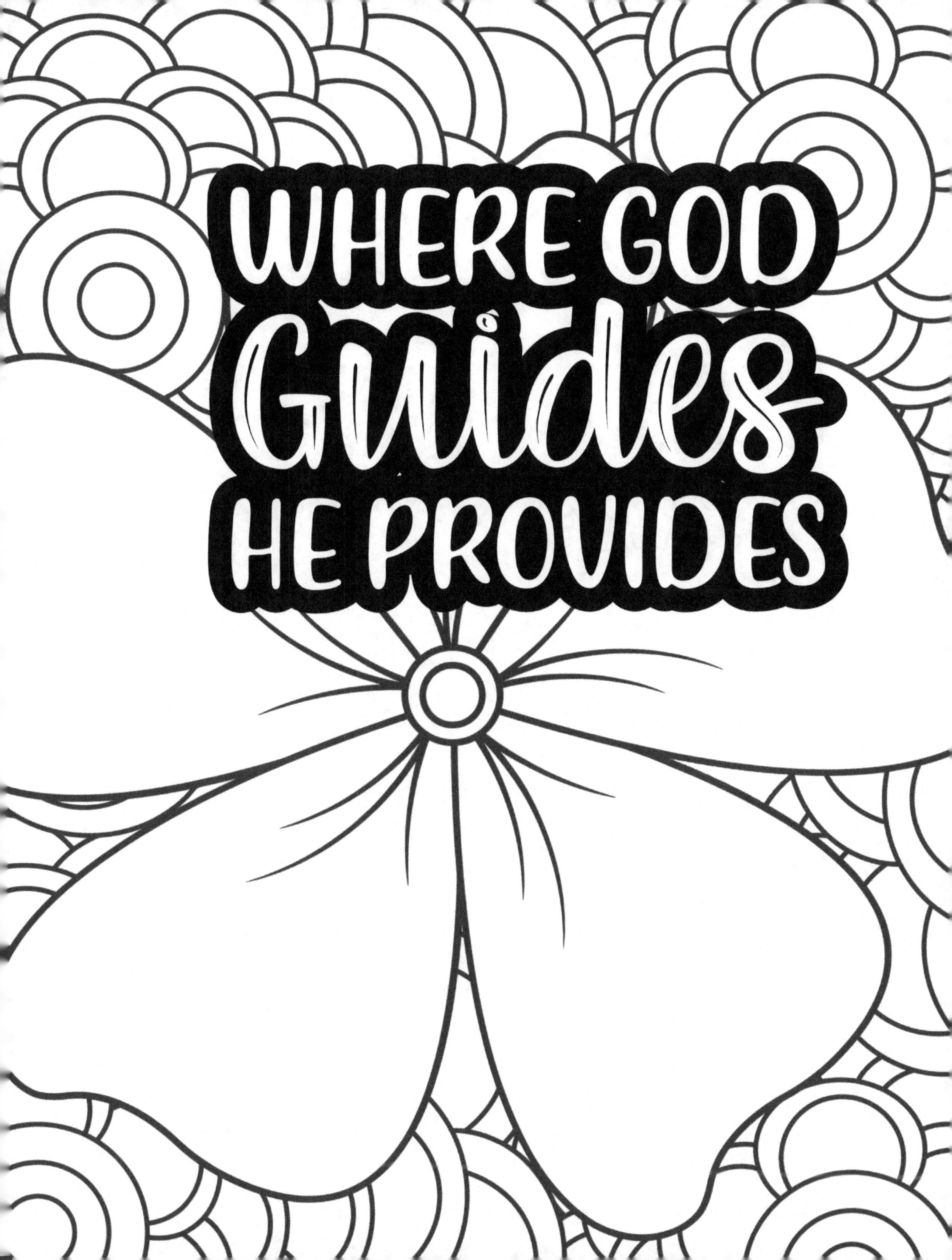
WHERE GOD
Guides
HE PROVIDES

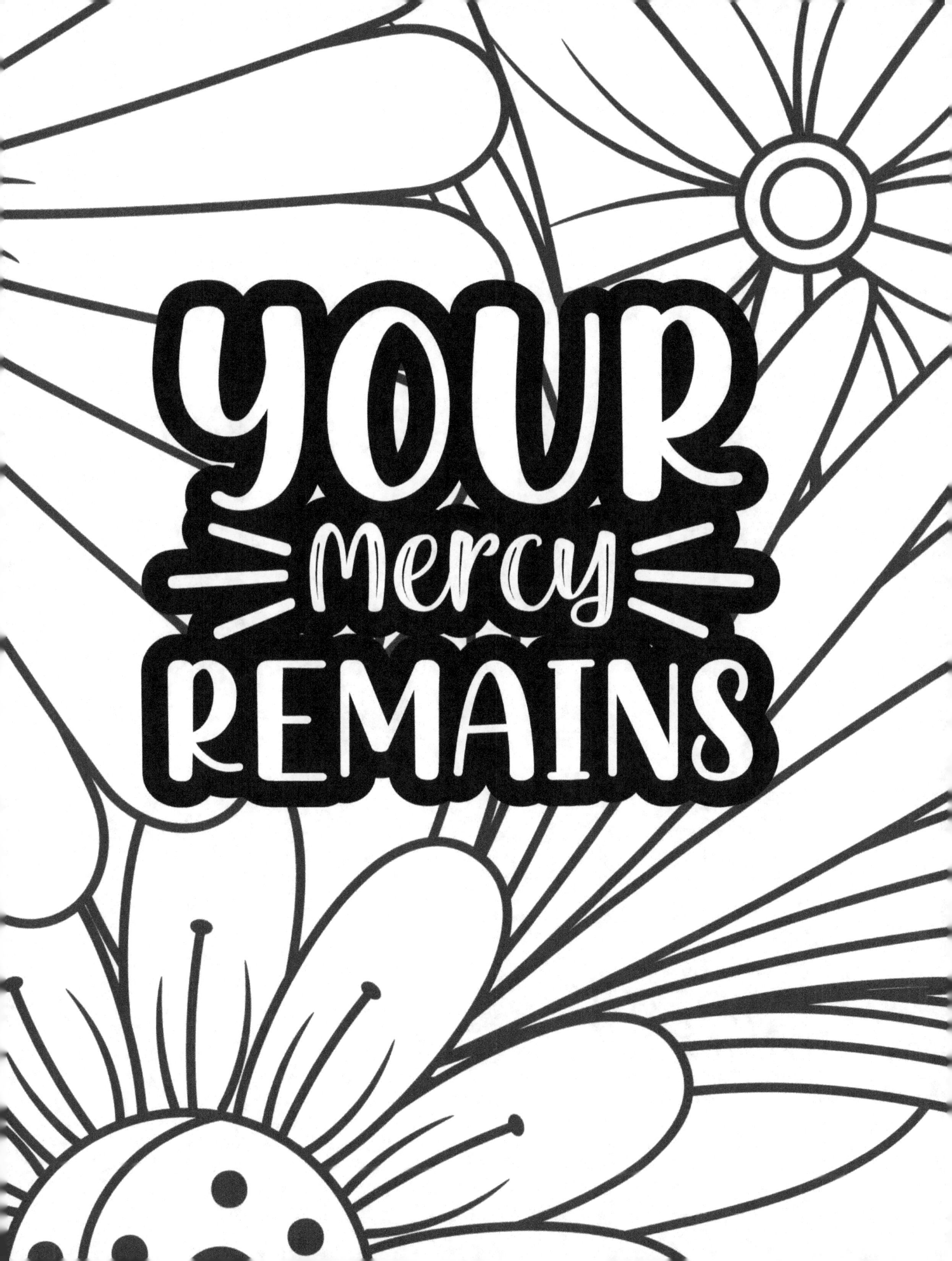
YOUR
mercy
REMAINS

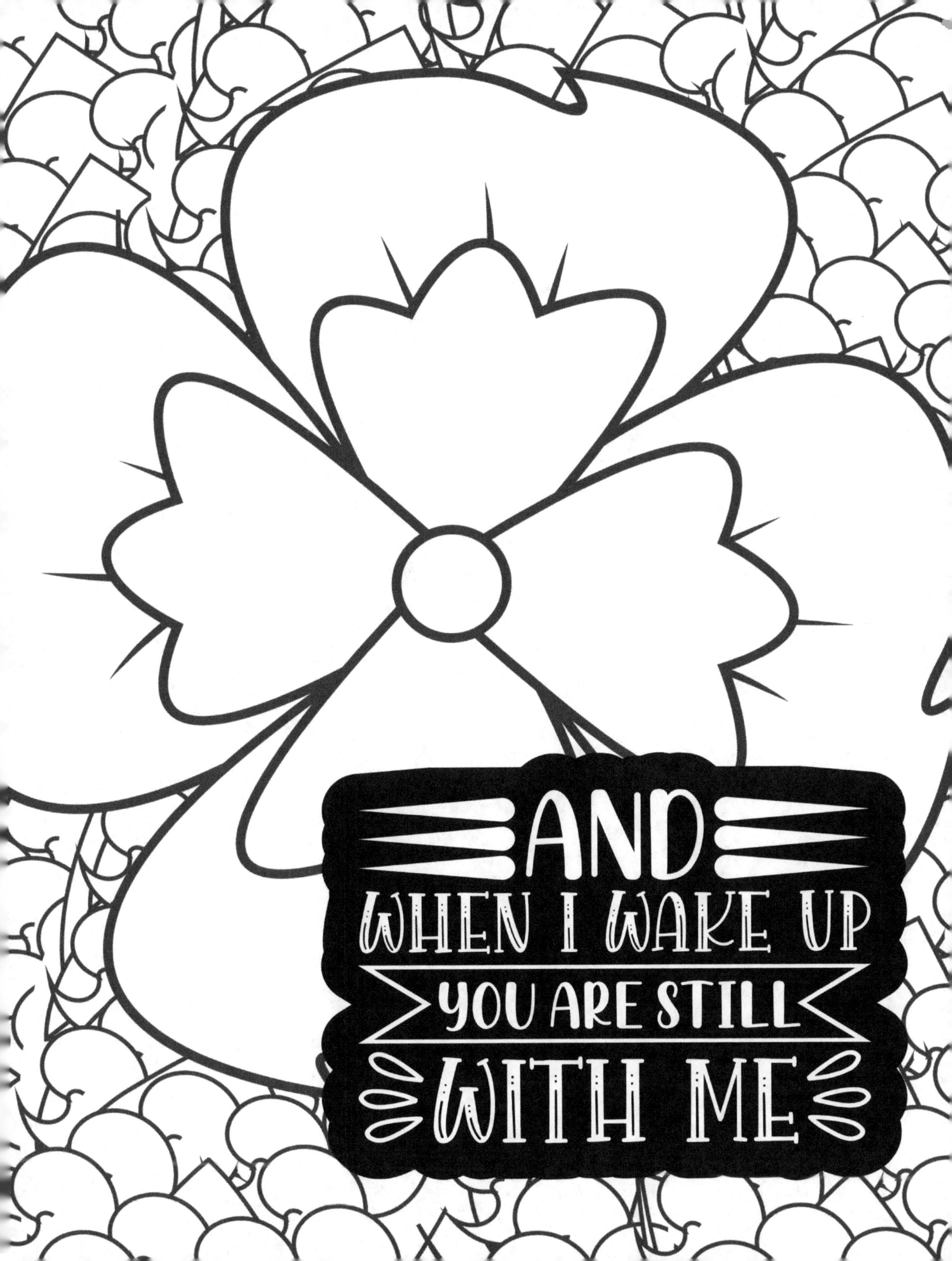
AND
WHEN I WAKE UP
YOU ARE STILL
WITH ME

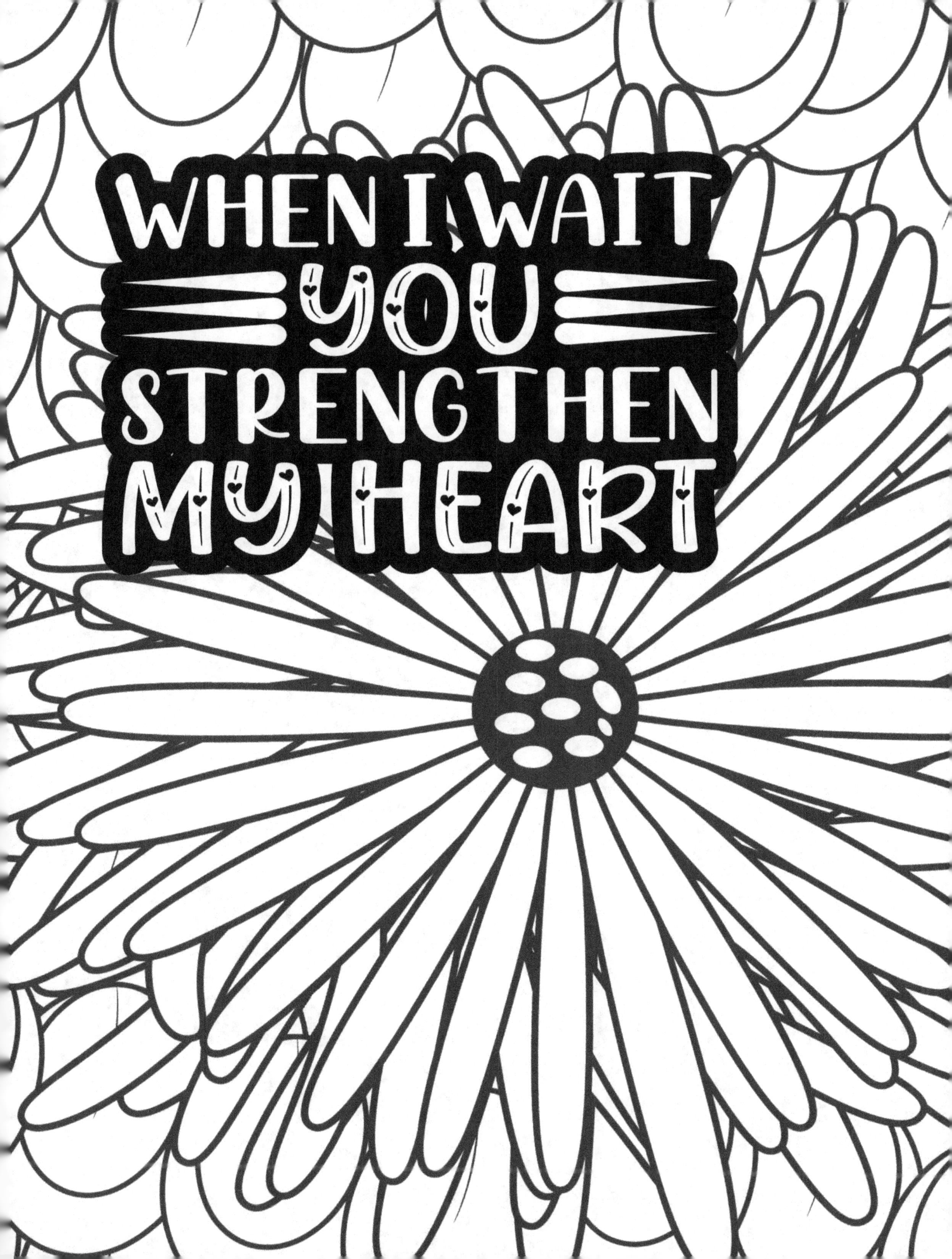
WHEN I WAIT
YOU
STRENGTHEN
MY HEART

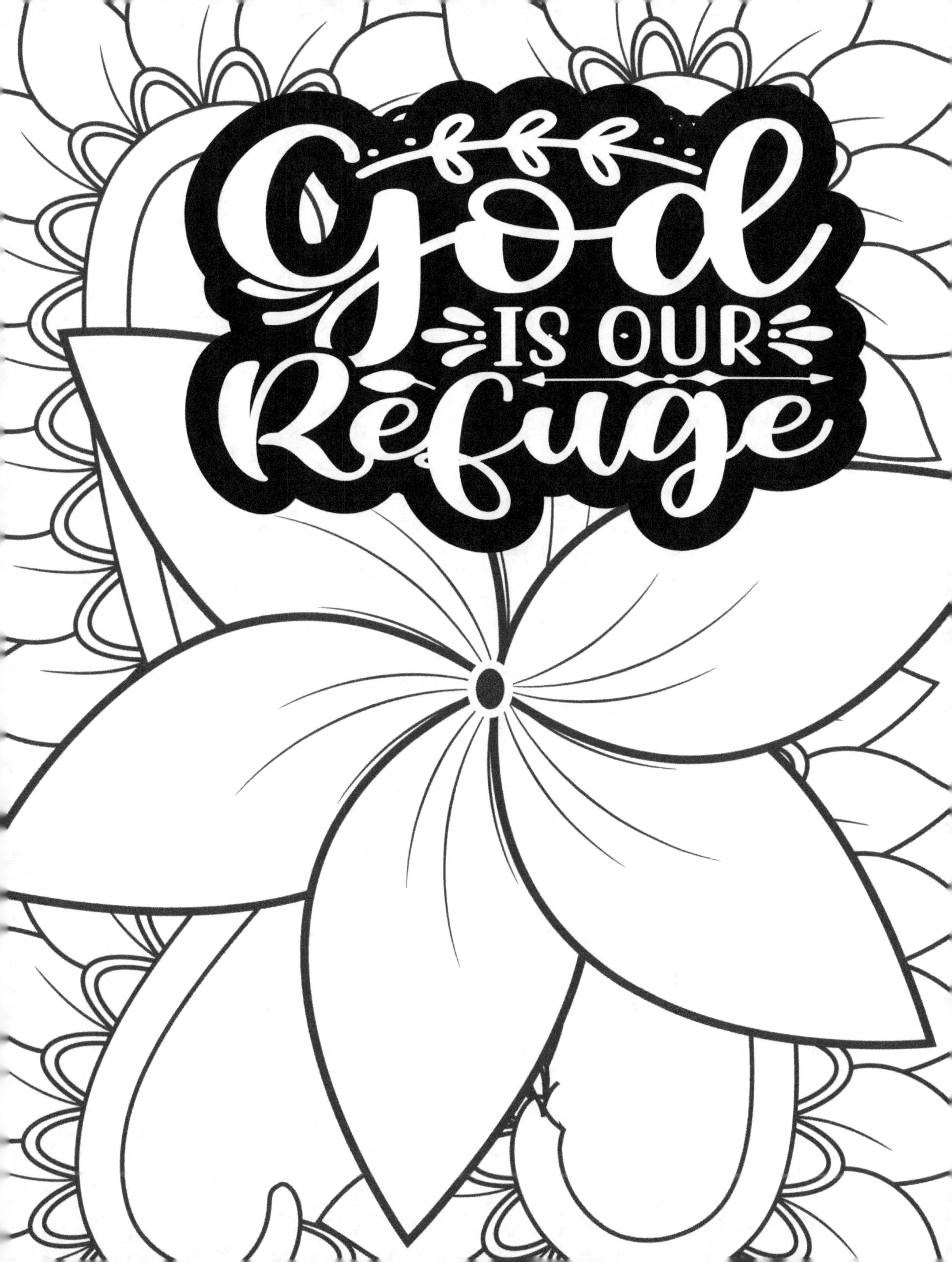
God
IS OUR
Refuge

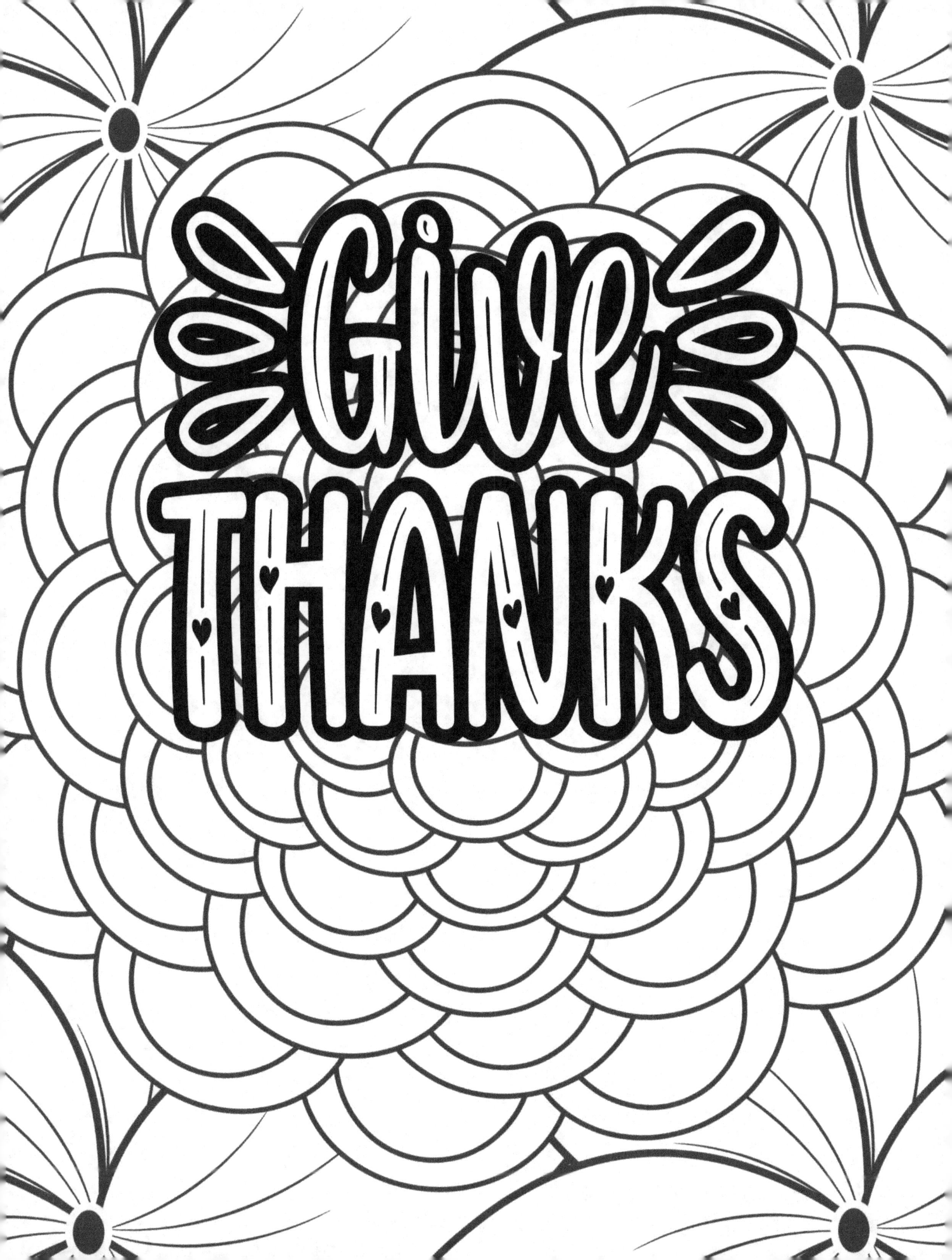
Give
THANKS

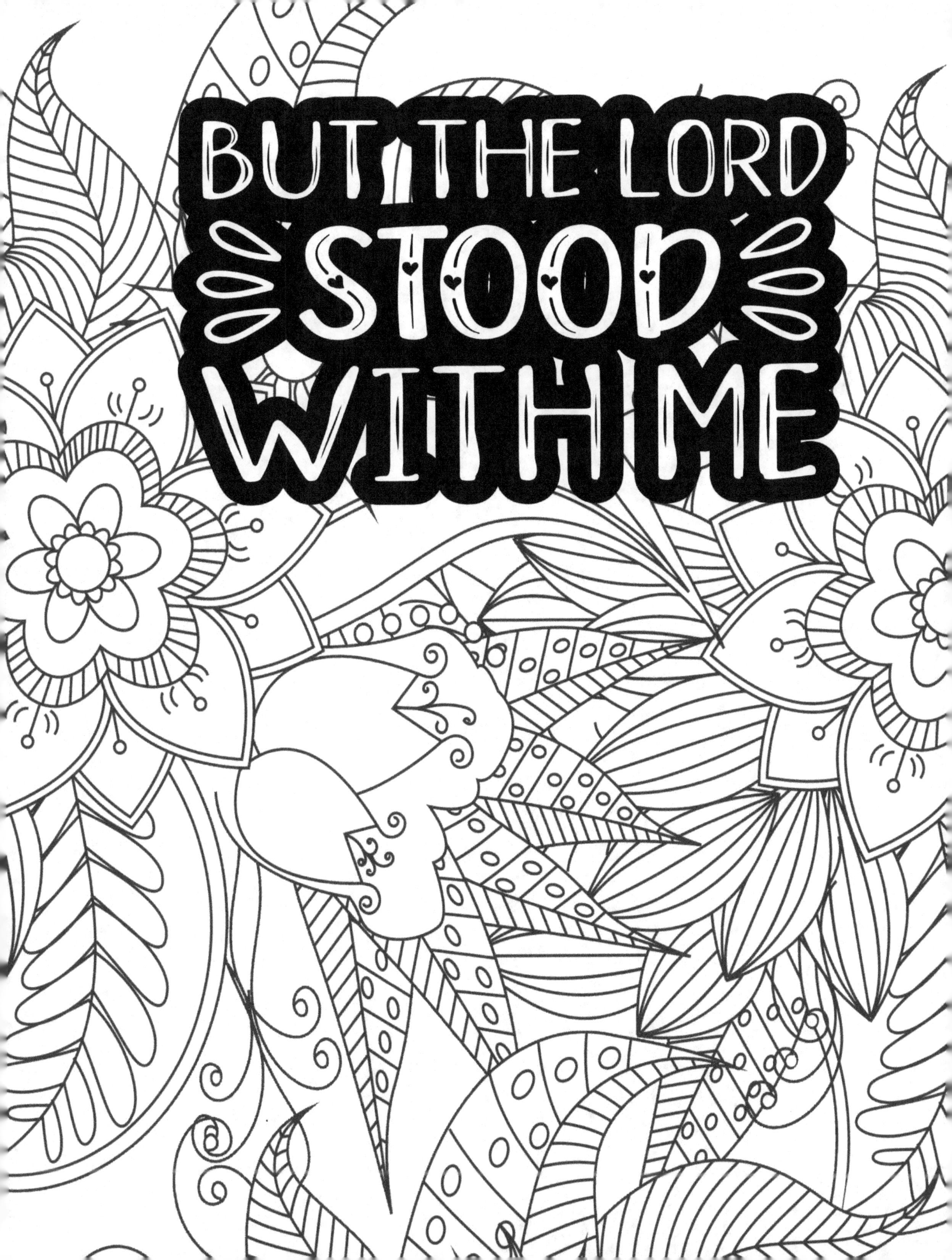
BUT THE LORD
STOOD
WITH ME

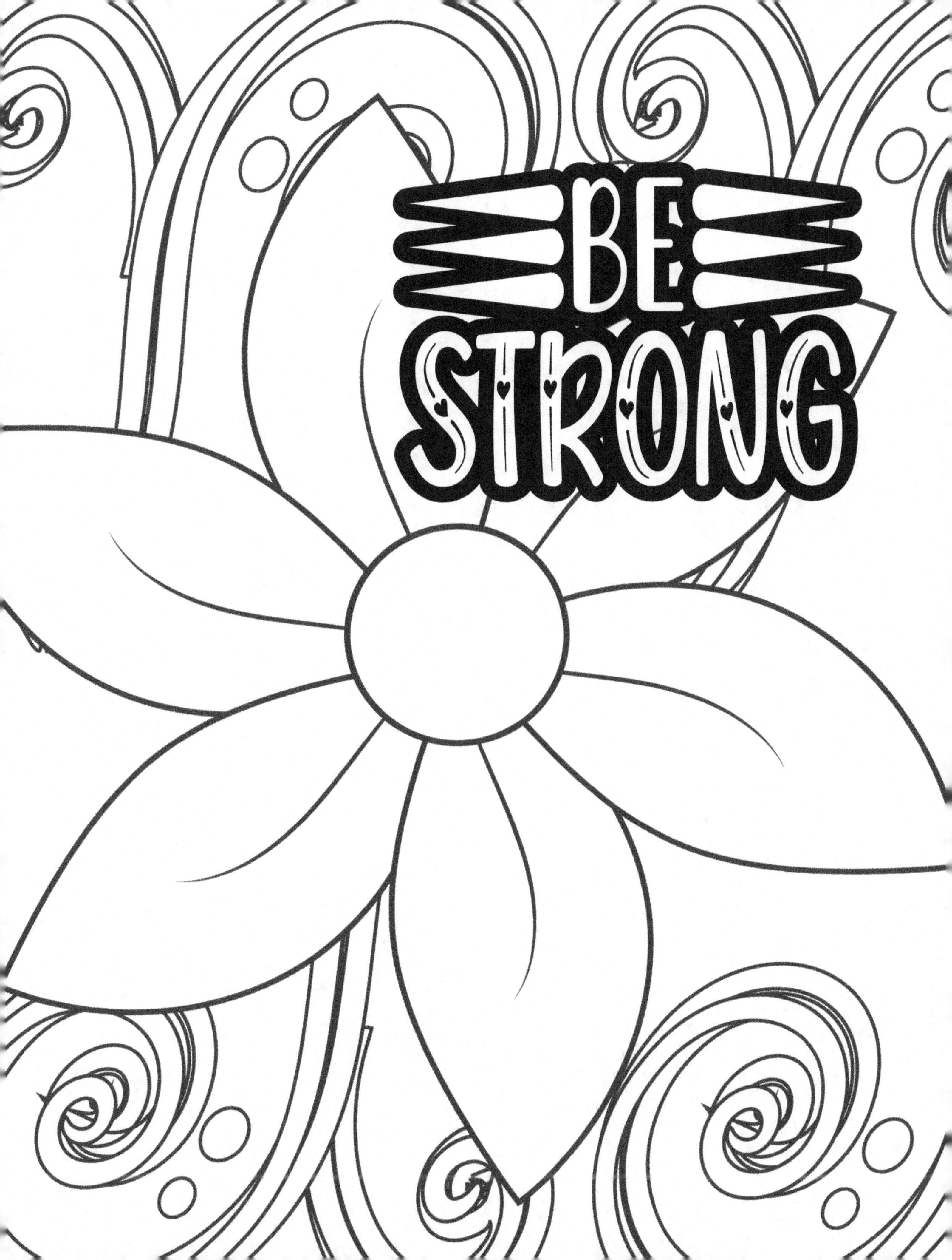
BE
STRONG

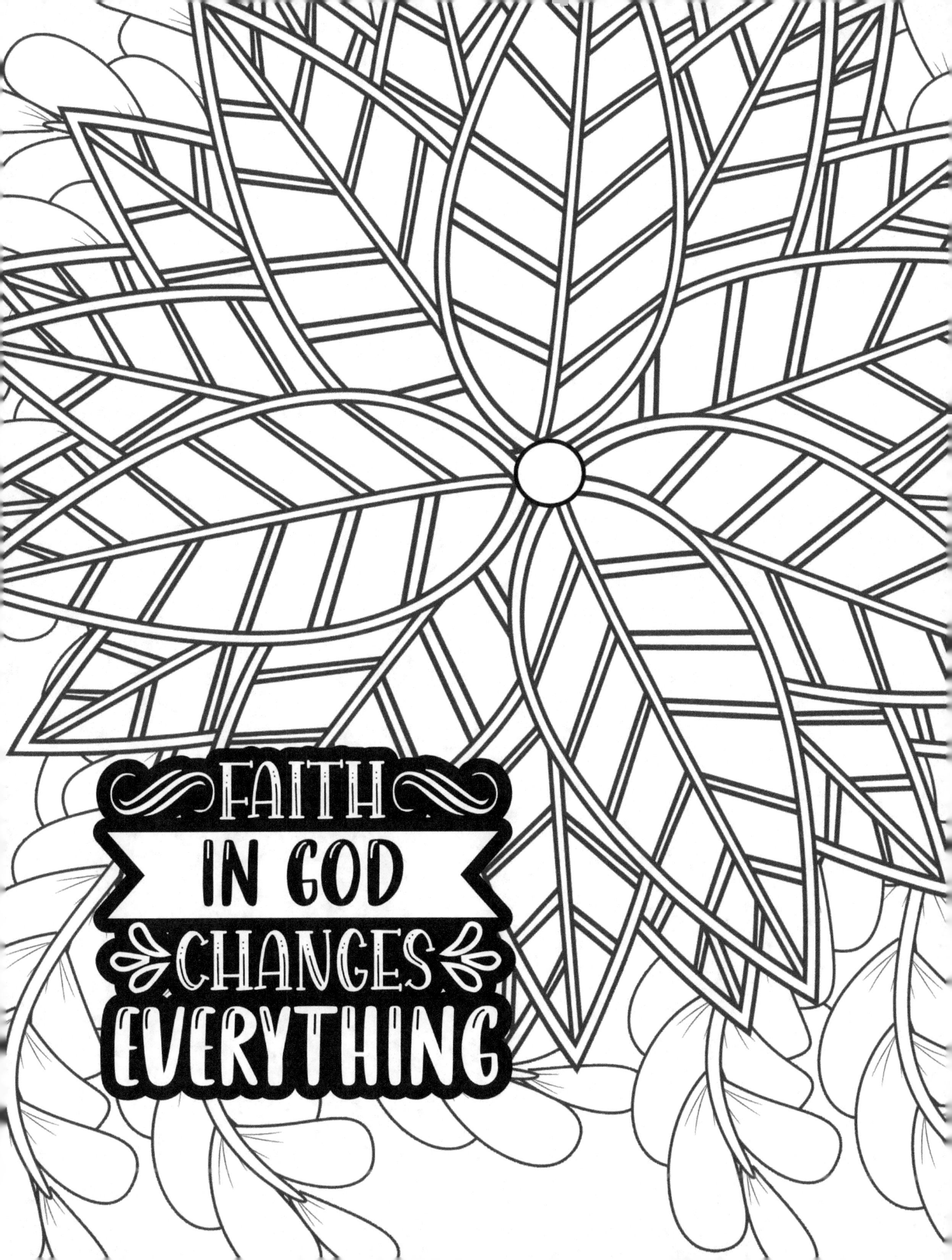
FAITH
IN GOD
CHANGES
EVERYTHING

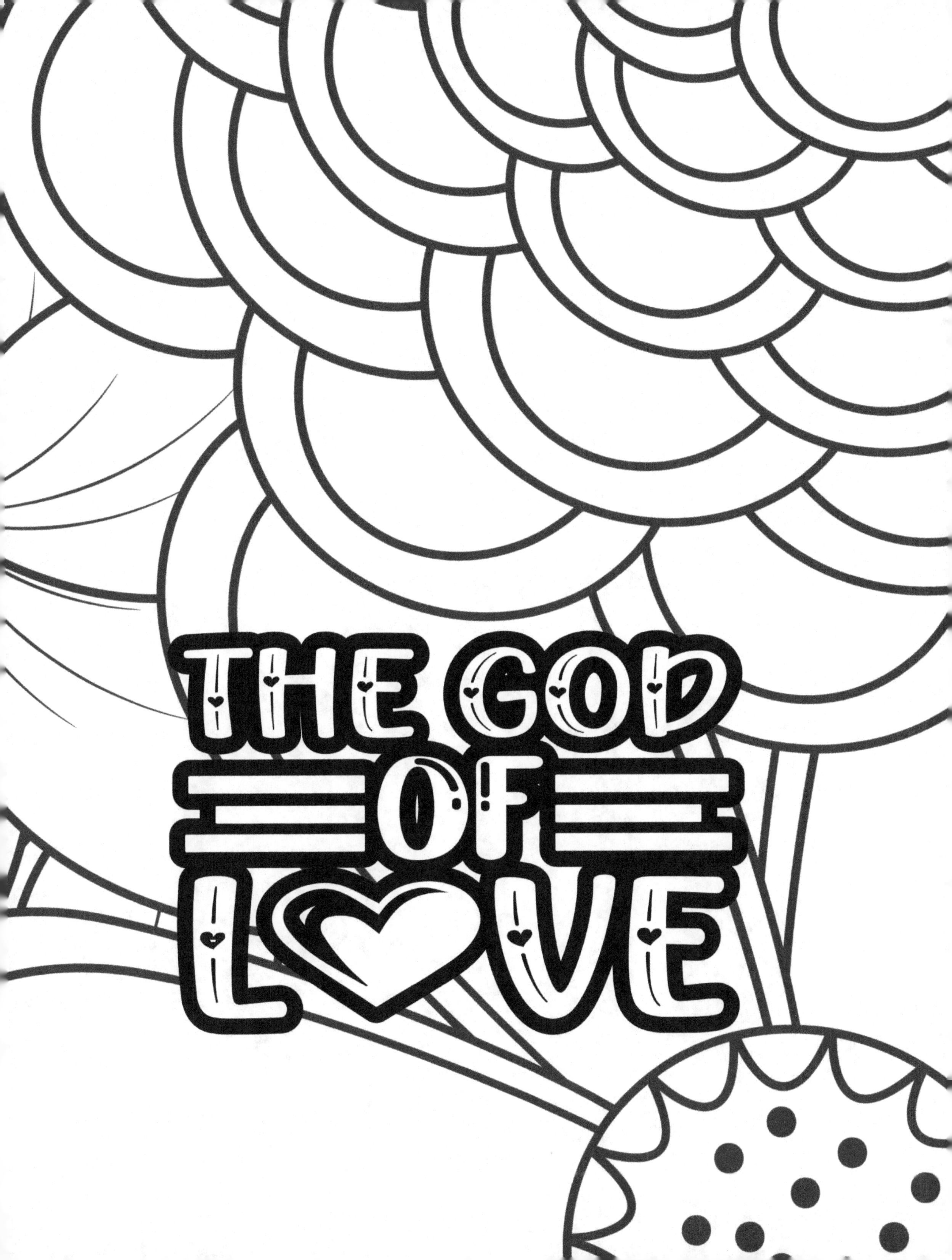
THE GOD
OF
LOVE

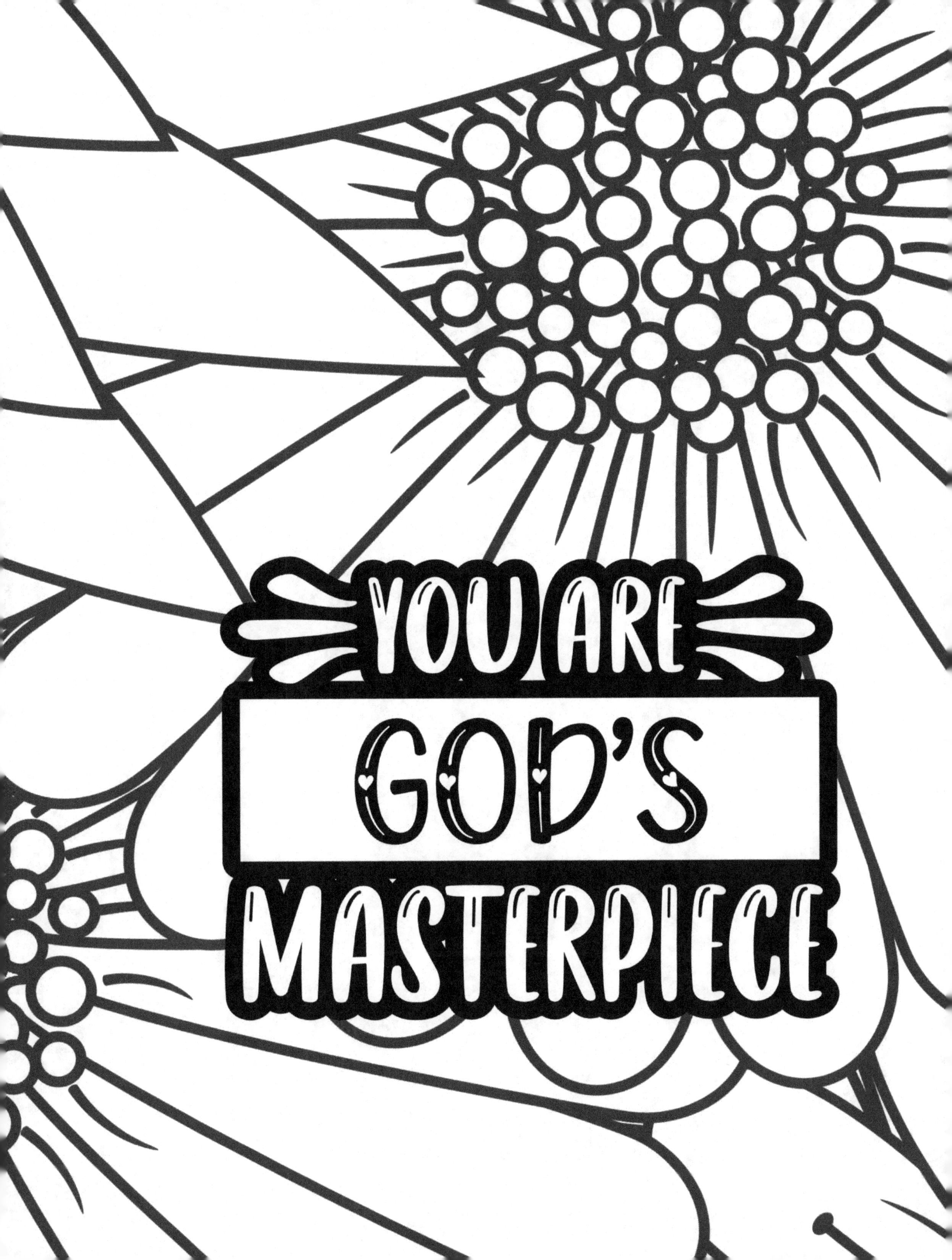
YOU ARE
GOD'S
MASTERPIECE

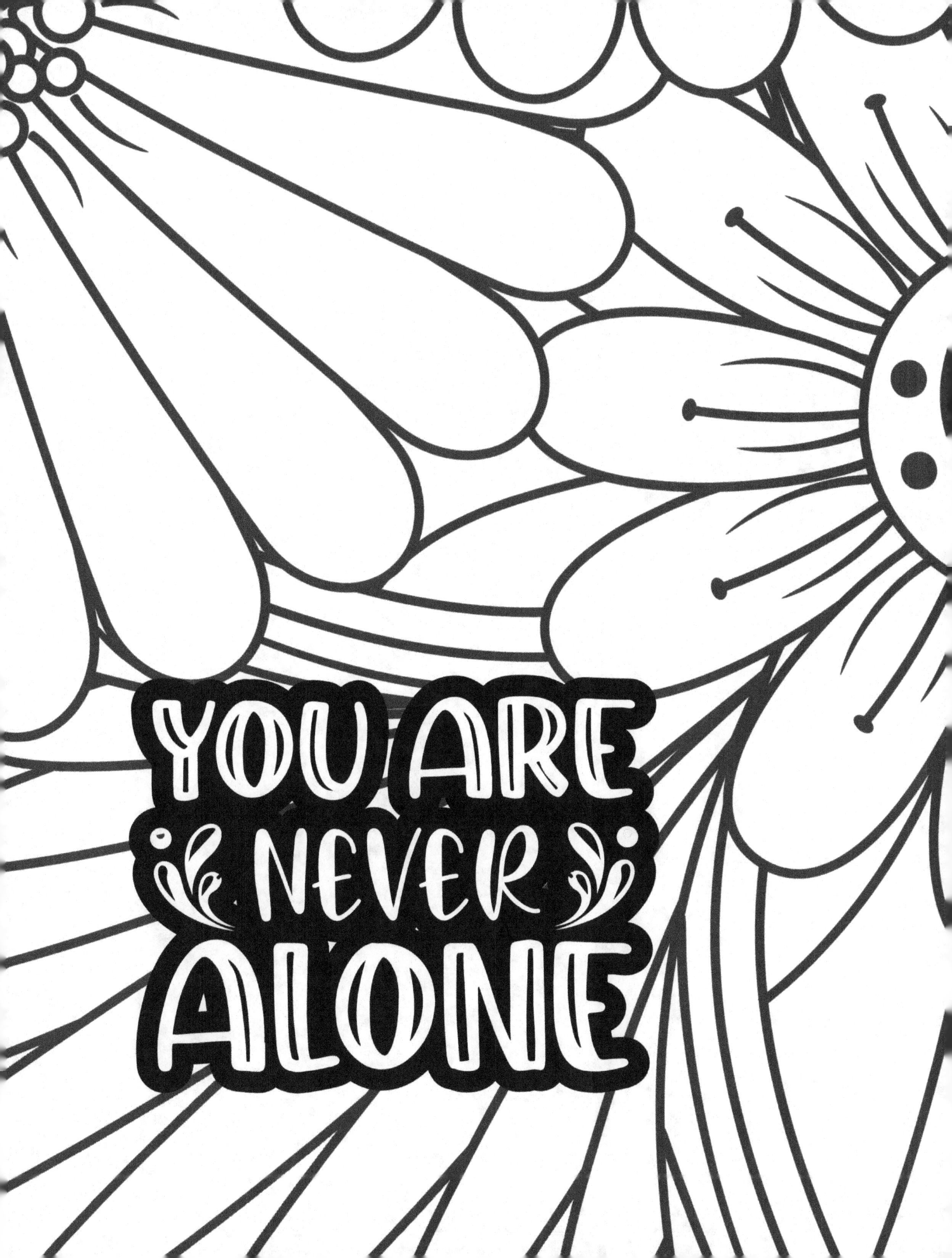
YOU ARE
NEVER
ALONE

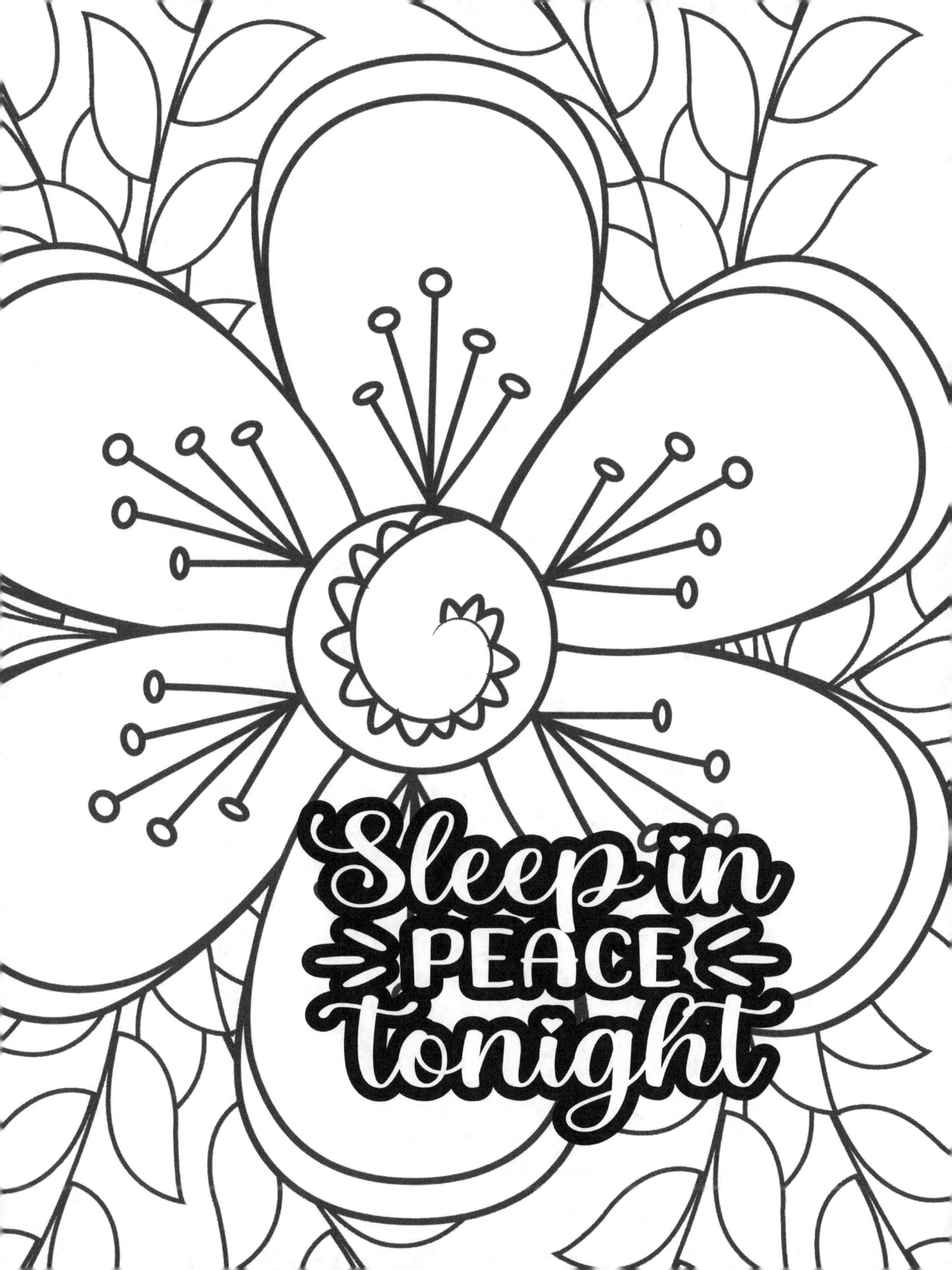
Sleep in
PEACE
tonight

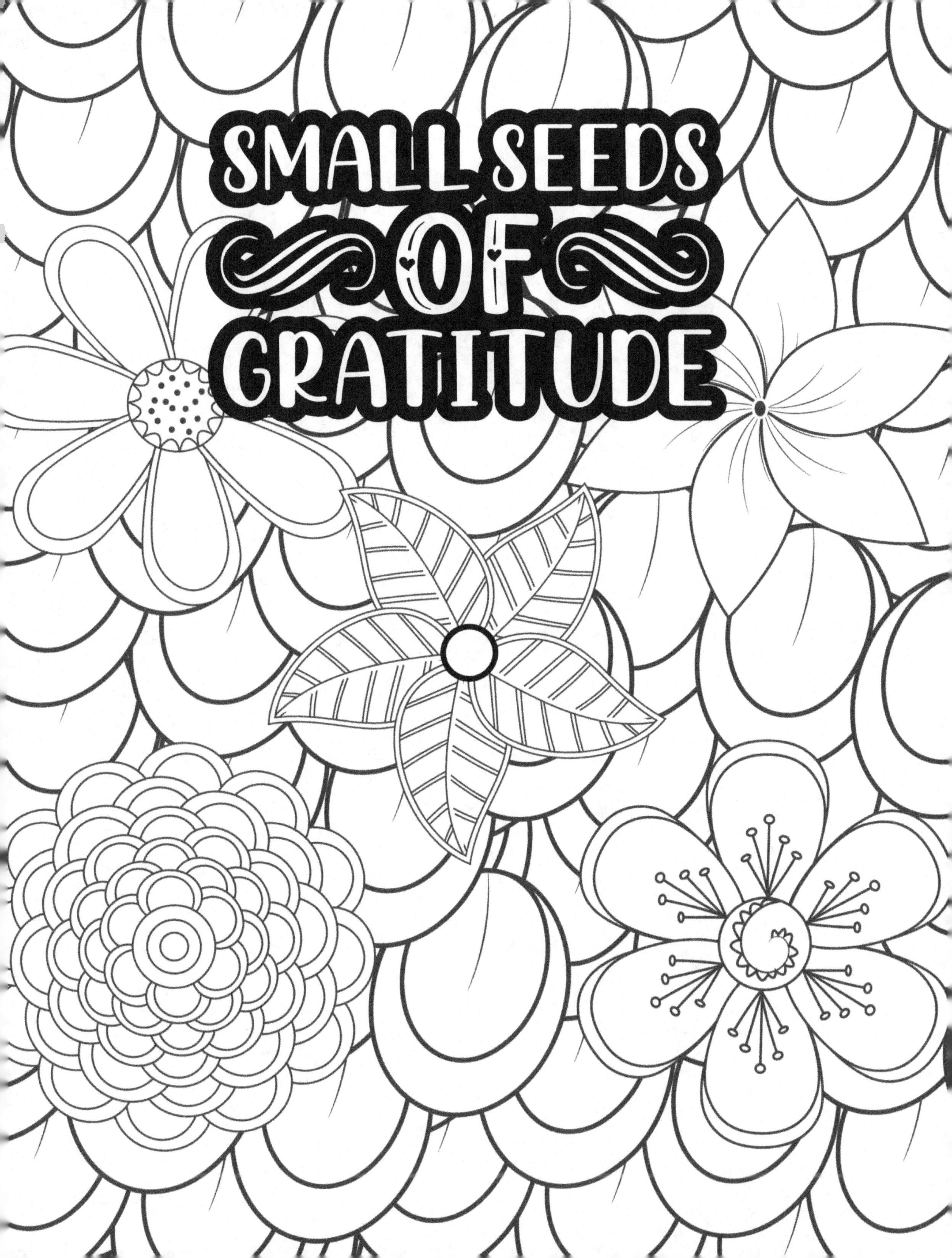
SMALL SEEDS
OF
GRATITUDE

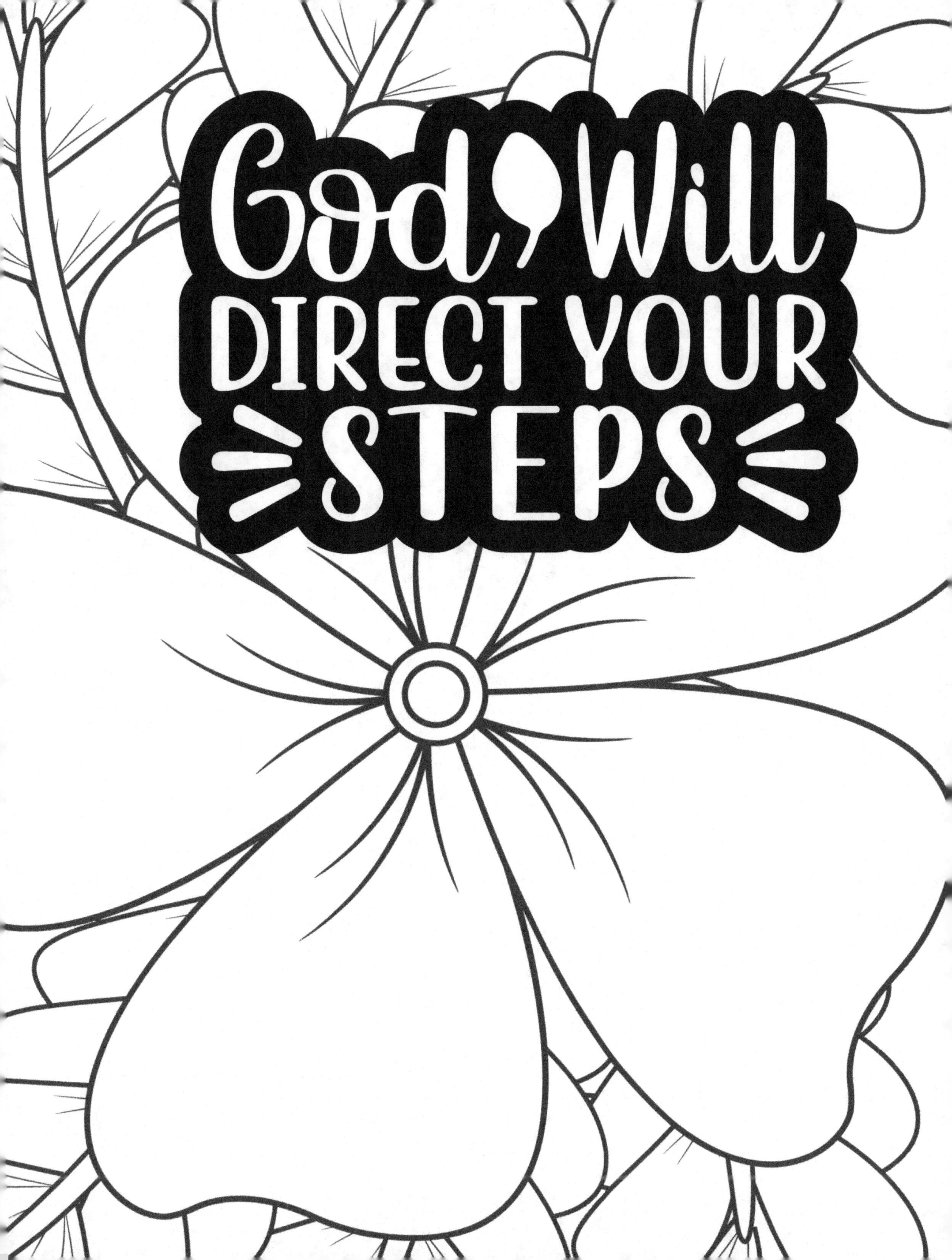
God Will
DIRECT YOUR
STEPS

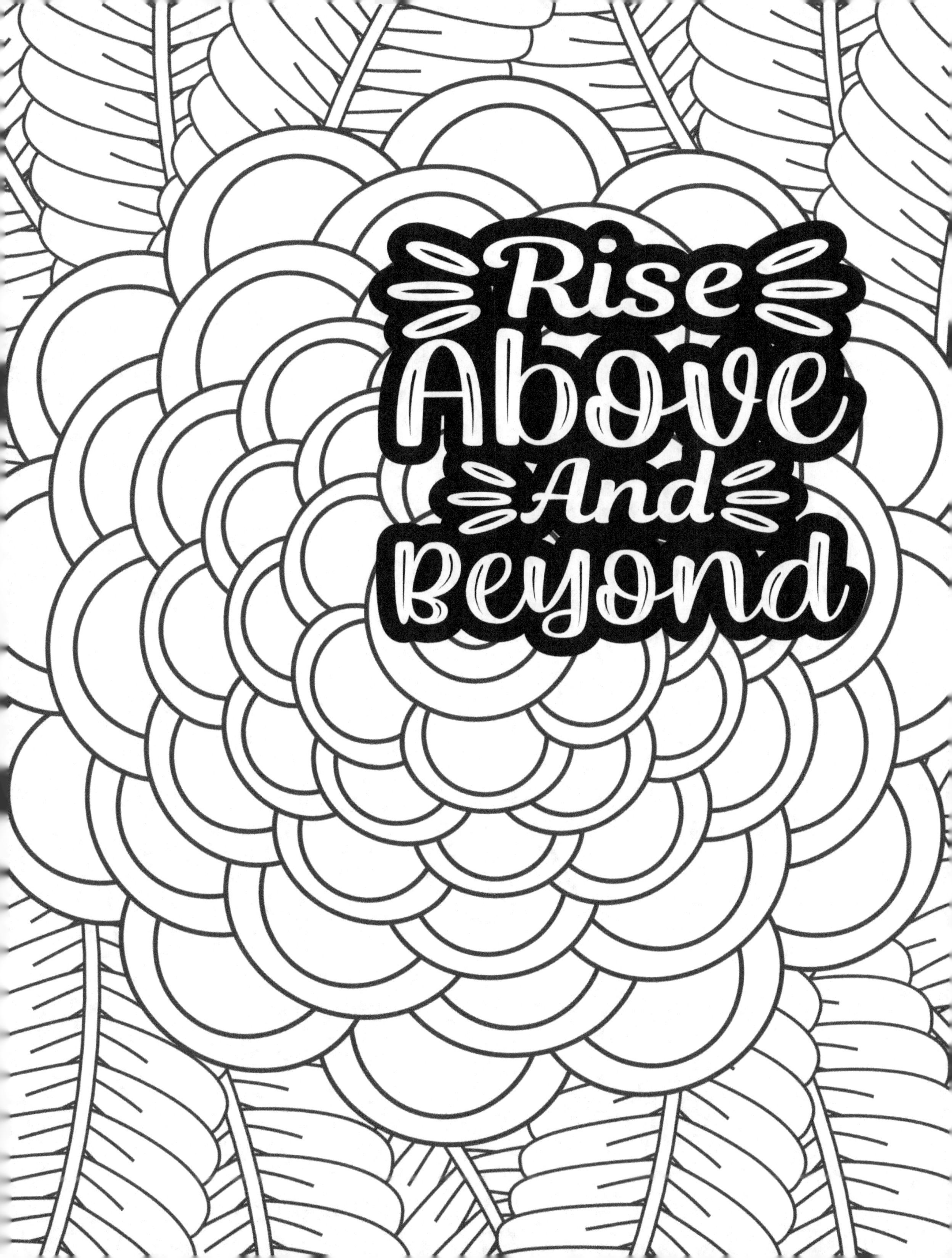
Rise
Above
And
Beyond

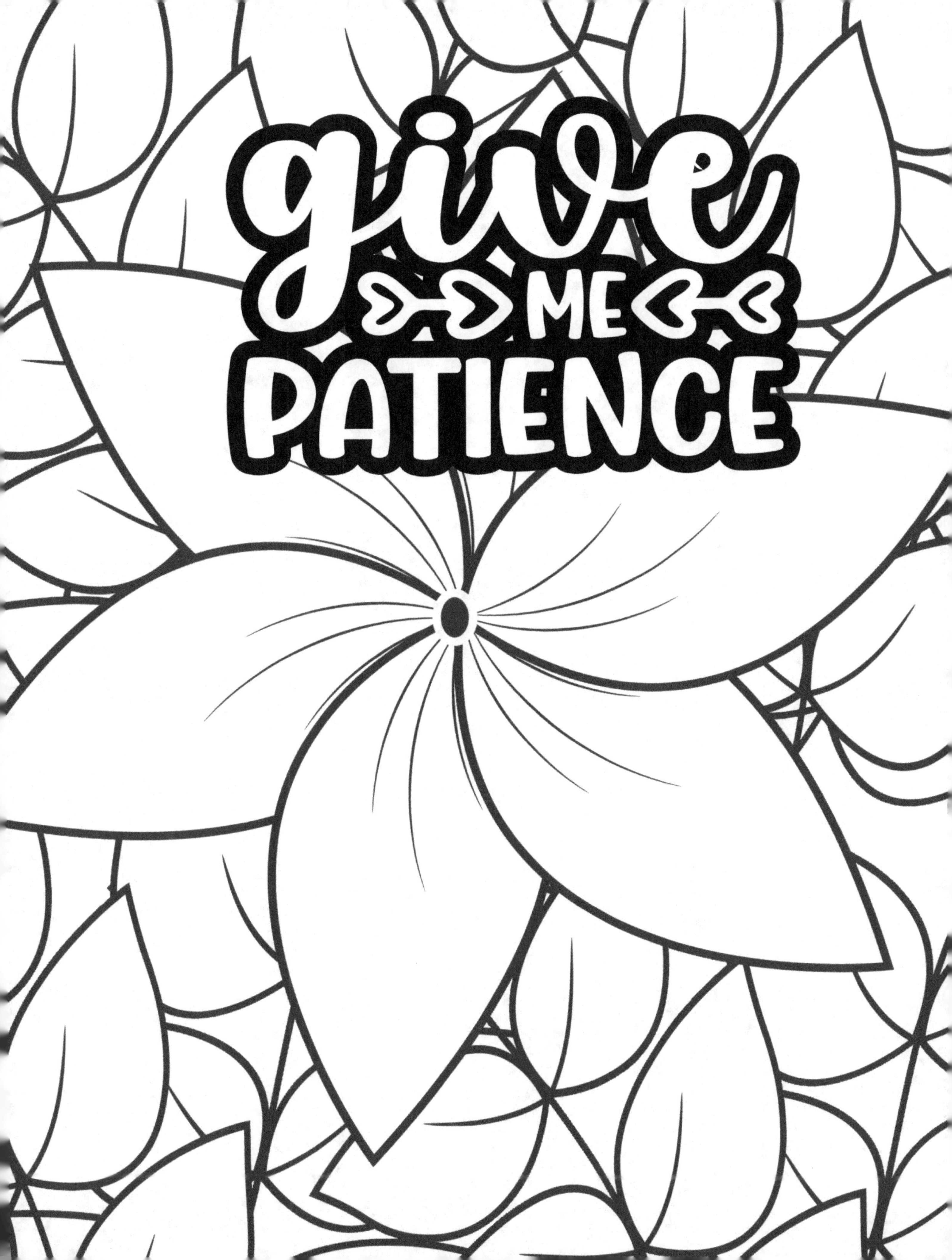
give
ME
PATIENCE

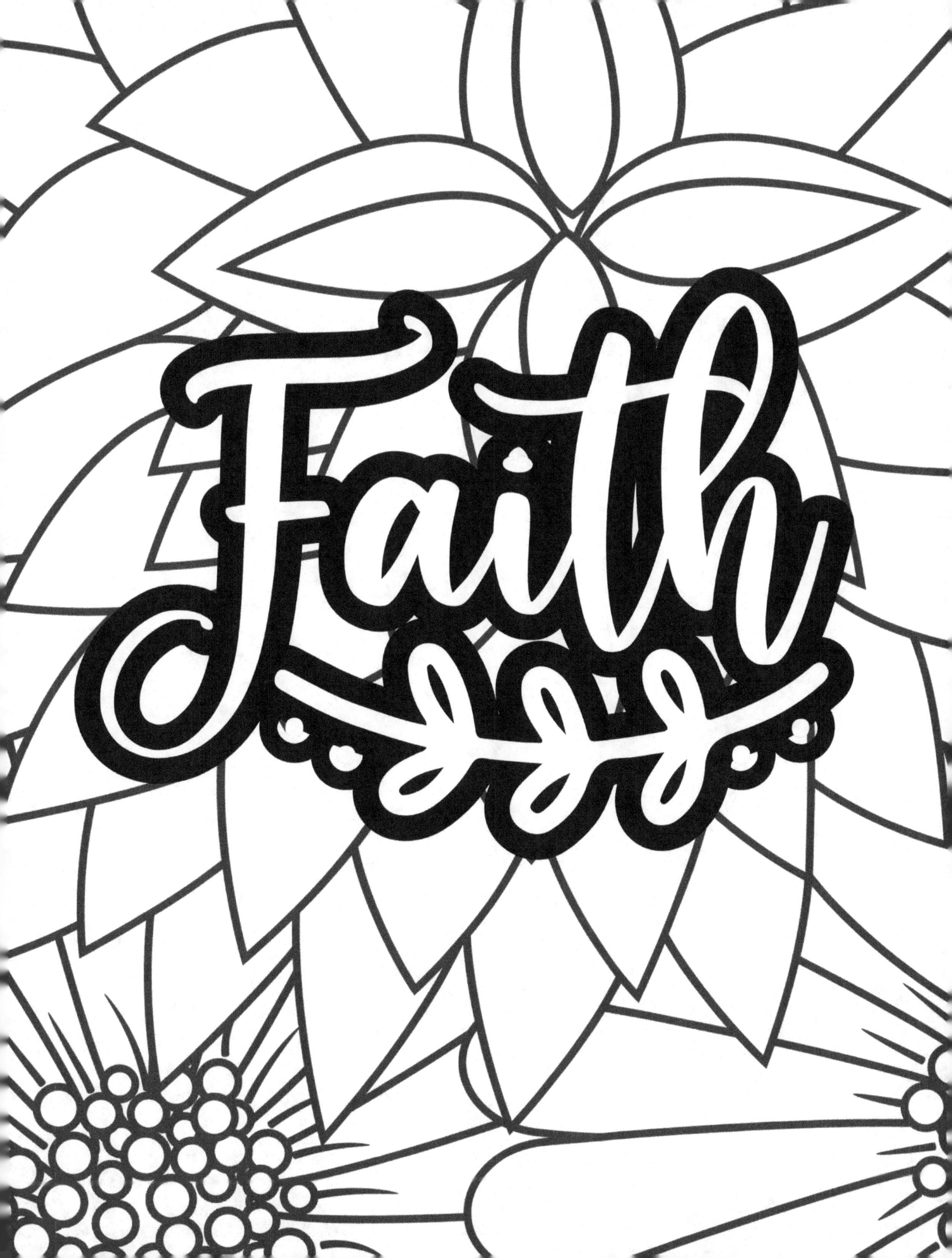
Faith

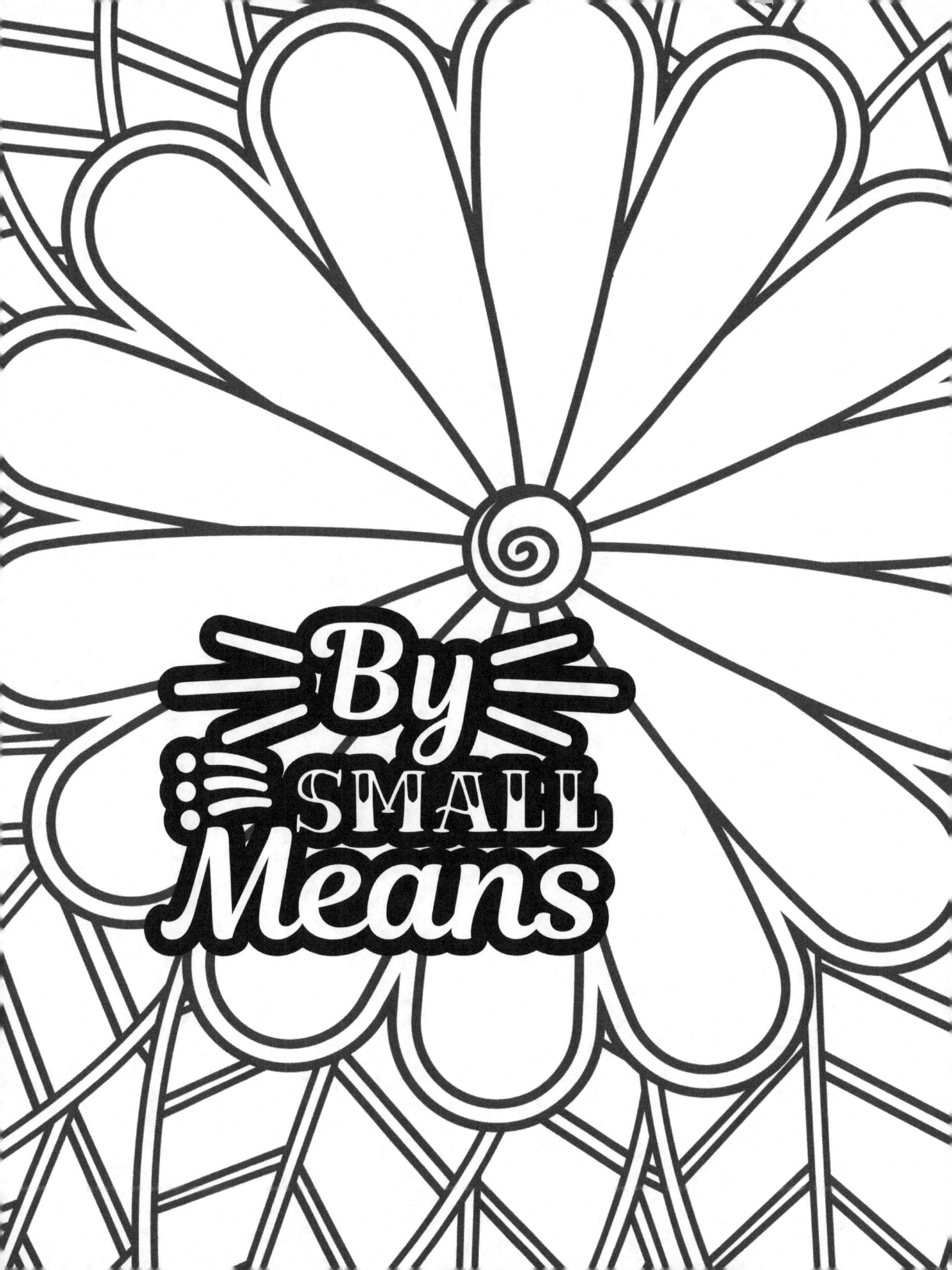
By
SMALL
Means

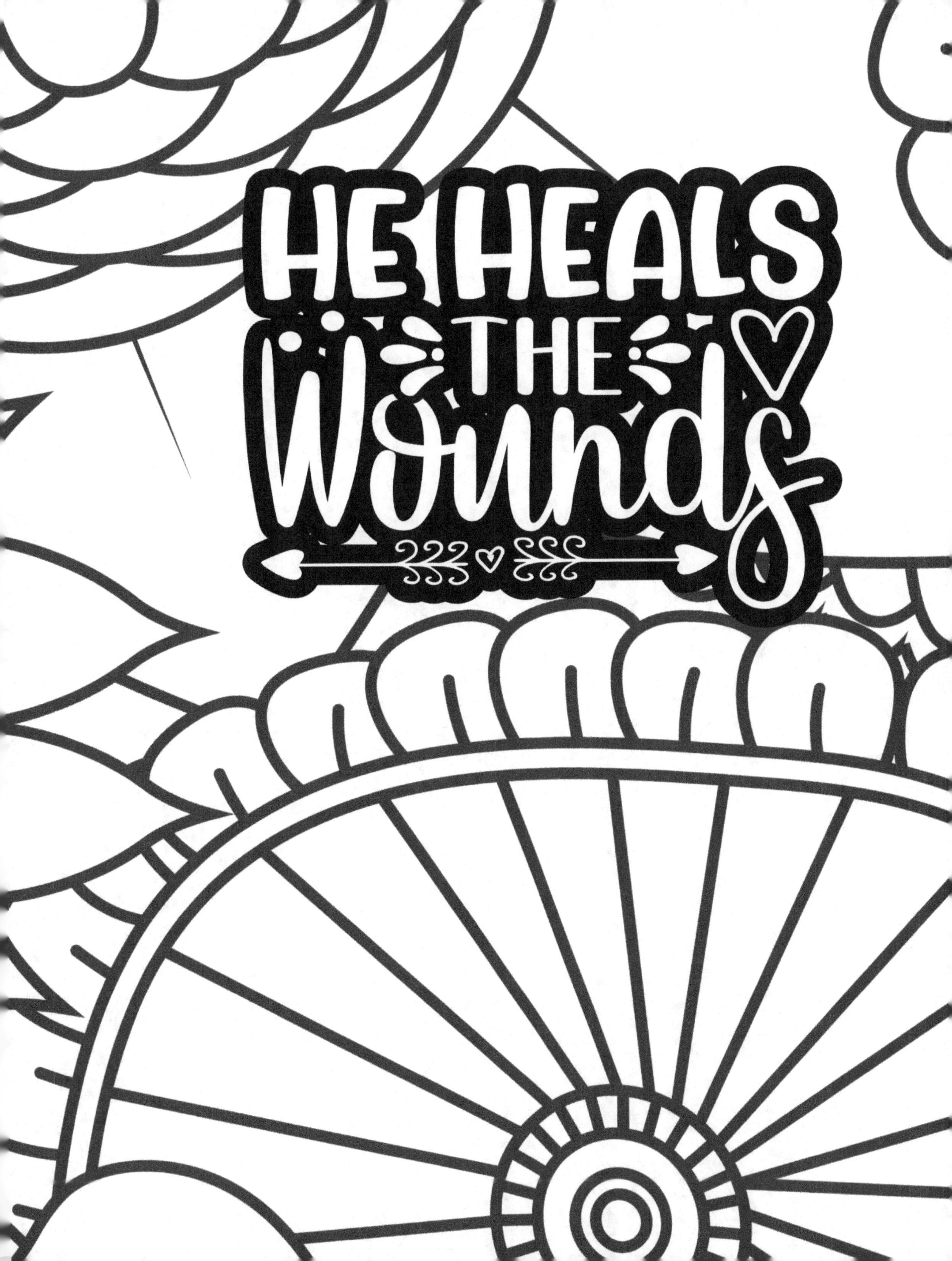
HE HEALS
THE
Wounds

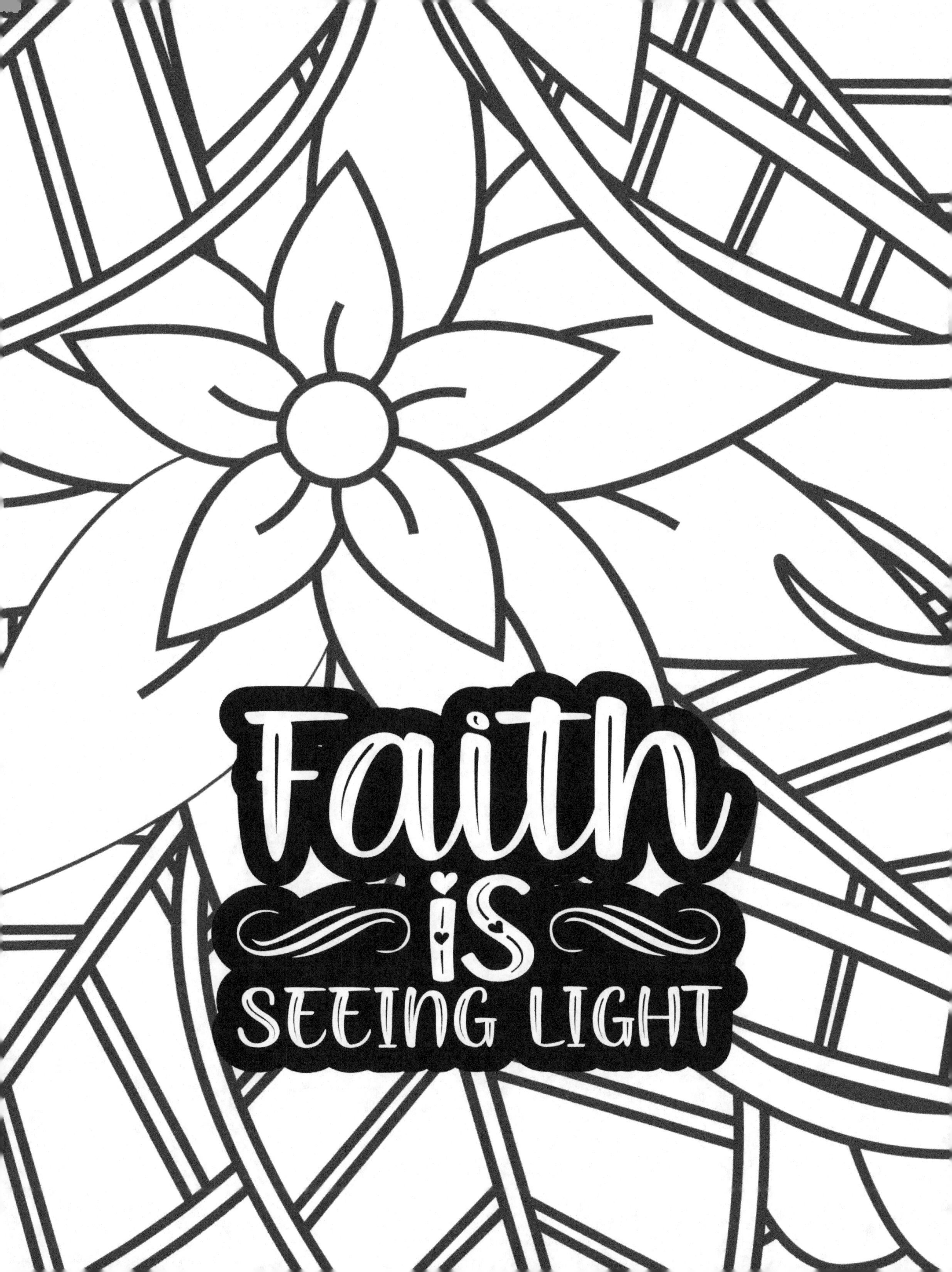
Faith
is
SEEING LIGHT

www.ingramcontent.com/pod-product-compliance
Lightning Source LLC
Chambersburg PA
CBHW080936220526
45465CB00008BA/3062
* 9 7 9 8 3 7 1 7 6 7 1 2 7 *